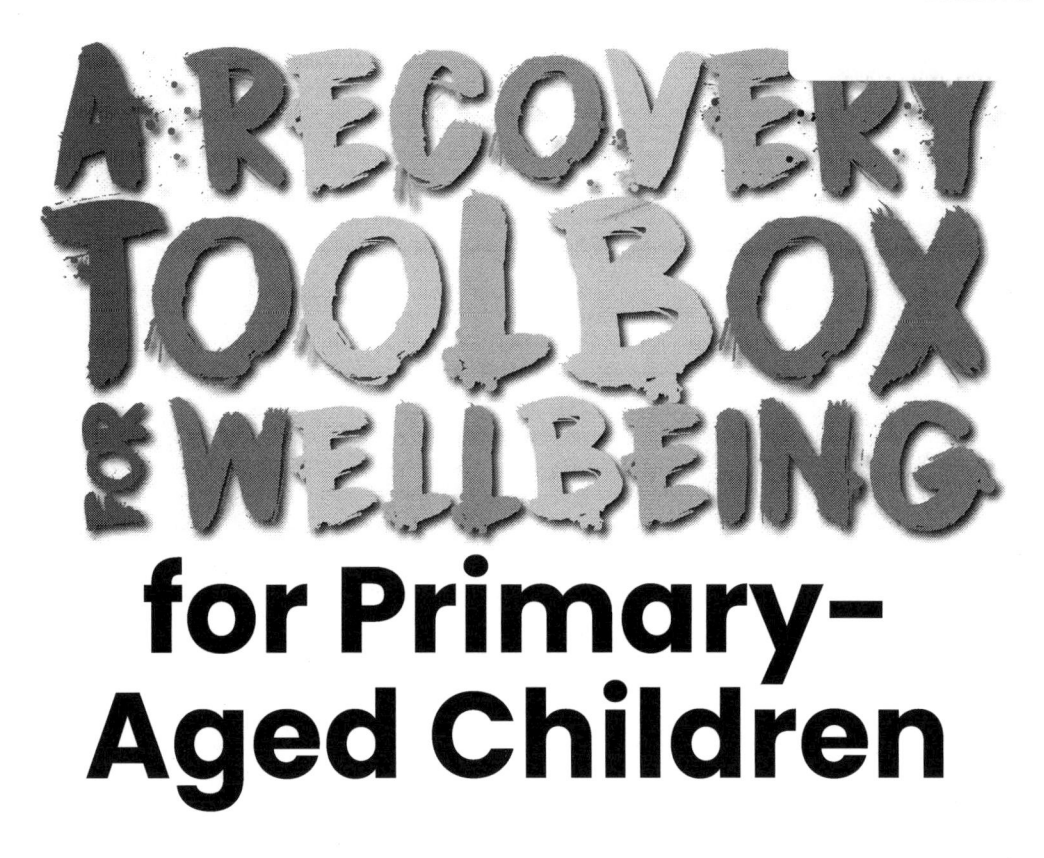

A RECOVERY TOOLBOX FOR WELLBEING
for Primary-Aged Children

The Toolbox of Wellbeing Series

A Toolbox of Wellbeing: Helpful strategies & activities for children, teens, their carers & teachers

A Recovery Toolbox for Wellbeing in the Early Years: Nurturing & wellbeing activities for children aged 3–6

A Recovery Toolbox for Primary-Aged Children: Nurturing & wellbeing activities for children aged 7–11

A Recovery Toolbox for Wellbeing for Adolescents & Teenagers: Nurturing & wellbeing activities for young people aged 12–16

My Toolbox of Wellbeing Journal: Creative, inspiring activities & strategies

A RECOVERY TOOLBOX FOR WELLBEING

for Primary Aged-Children

Nurturing & Wellbeing Activities for Children Aged 7-11

Tina Rae & Ali D'Amario

HINTON HOUSE Essentials

First published in 2021 by
Hinton House Publishers Ltd
T +44 (0)1280 822557 E info@hintonpublishers.com

www.hintonpublishers.com

© 2021 Tina Rae & Alison D'Amario

The right of Tina Rae and Alison D'Amario to be identified as authors of this Work has been asserted by them in accordance with sections 77 and 78 of the Copyright, Designs and Patents Act 1988.

All rights reserved. The whole of this work including texts and illustrations is protected by copyright. No part of it may be copied, altered, adapted or otherwise exploited in any way without express prior permission, except in accordance with the provisions of the Copyright, Designs and Patents Act 1988 or in order to photocopy or make duplicating masters of those pages so indicated, without alteration and including copyright notices, for the express purpose of instruction and examination. No parts of this work may otherwise be loaded, stored, manipulated, reproduced, or transmitted in any form or by any means, electronic or mechanical, including photocopying or storing it in any information, storage or retrieval system, without prior written permission from the publisher, on behalf of the copyright owner.

Warning: The doing of an unauthorised act in relation to a copyright work may result in both a civil claim for damages and criminal prosecution.

British Library Cataloguing in Publication Data
A CIP catalogue record for this book is available from the British Library.

ISBN 978 1 912112 52 4

Printed and bound in the United Kingdom

Contents

Preface ix
About the author xiii

Introduction 1
    Why We Wrote this Book 1
    What is Emotional & Psychological Trauma? 4
    Protecting the Mental Health of Children after Trauma 4
    How Children React to Emotional & Psychological Trauma 9
    Using the Recovery Toolbox 10

1 Self-Regulation Activities 13
    1.1 Square Breathing 14
    1.2 Hand Breathing 15
    1.3 Anger Iceberg 16
    1.4 Grounding the Senses 17
    1.5 Mindful Eating 18
    1.6 Mindful Clapping 19
    1.7 Visualisation 20
    1.8 Body Scanning Script 21
    1.9 Calming Positions 22
    1.10 Regulate the Senses 23

2 Resilience-Building Activities 25
    2.1 Positive Diary 26
    2.2 Times that I Have Been Brave 27
    2.3 My Coping Strategies 28
    2.4 Who Can You Talk To? 29
    2.5 Self-Care Checklist 30
    2.6 My Box of Things to Look Forward To 31
    2.7 Friendly Talk for Building Resilience 32
    2.8 Bin It! 33
    2.9 Positive Traits 34
    2.10 True Grit! 35

3 Self-Esteem & Social Skills Activities 37
   3.1   All About Me 39
   3.2   Confidence Boosters 40
   3.3   My Amazing Body 41
   3.4   I Am Special 42
   3.5   Things that I Like About Me 43
   3.6   Strengths Cards 44
   3.7   Friendship Definitions! 45
   3.8   Building Friendship Skills 46
   3.9   Managing Conflict 48
   3.10 Coping with Conflict 49

4 Effective Thinking Activities 51
   4.1   Know Yourself! 55
   4.2   Comfortable Feelings Daily Diary 56
   4.3   My ABC 58
   4.4   Positive Acts 59
   4.5   Controlling Thoughts 60
   4.6   Thought Detective 1 61
   4.7   Thought Detective 2: Friends Can Help! 62
   4.8   'What Ifs' Game 63
   4.9   Good Decisions for a Positive Future 64
   4.10 Making a Priority Goal for My Positive Future! 65

5 Anxiety-Busting Activities 67
   5.1   Body Outline 70
   5.2   My Worries 71
   5.3   Things that I Can Control 72
   5.4   Hidden Feelings 73
   5.5   Anxiety Checklist! 74
   5.6   Calming Cards 75
   5.7   Scaling 76
   5.8   Worry Eaters! 77
   5.9   Exercise Reduces Anxiety! 78
   5.10 My Anxiety Playlist 79

6 Transition Activities ... 81
- 6.1 Coming Back to School ... 82
- 6.2 Change is Good! ... 83
- 6.3 Problem Postcards ... 84
- 6.4 Scale It! ... 86
- 6.5 Changes: I Can Cope with Them! ... 87
- 6.6 Connecting with Others ... 88
- 6.7 A Positive Note to Me ... 89
- 6.8 Personal Information for My Teachers ... 90
- 6.9 Safe Haven ... 91
- 6.10 My Best Future ... 92

Appendices ... 93
- 1 Helpful Websites ... 94
- 2 Mindfulness Information ... 96
- 3 Stress, Anxiety Disorders & Depression Information ... 99
- 4 Emotion Coaching Information ... 104
- 5 Using Circle of Friends Approaches ... 106
- 6 Trauma Recovery Self-Care Tips ... 110
- 7 Whole-School Recovery ... 113
- 8 A Recovery Plan to Support School Staff and Carers as Children Return to School ... 116

References ... 118

Preface

Never has there been a time when knowing how to manage your own wellbeing and how to support our children in doing this has been so vital.

Tina Rae (2020)

At the time of writing this series of books we are in the middle of a global pandemic and many researchers across the world are warning that this coronavirus pandemic could inflict long-lasting emotional trauma on an unprecedented global scale. They assert that it could leave millions wrestling with debilitating psychological disorders, while dashing hopes for a swift economic recovery. The COVID-19 crisis has combined mental health stressors that have been studied before in other disasters, but which have never been seen consolidated in one global crisis.

It has left millions without jobs, sent billions into isolation and forced nearly everyone on earth to grapple with the feeling that they or those they love are suddenly physically vulnerable. The nature of the disease means that there can be no certainty about when the worst will pass. Hundreds of thousands have been infected, thousands have died, the virus continues to spread, and a vaccine for everyone on this planet could be more than a year away.

The scale of this outbreak as a traumatic event is almost beyond our comprehension as, unlike previous disasters such as 9/11 or World War 2, during which the anxiety caused was limited by geography, there are now no boundaries. Trying to understand this is difficult when the available research on how humans cope with such events covers how humans cope with quarantine, mass disasters and ongoing stressors, but not with all three simultaneously.

The concern of governments around the world is also focused on financial recovery options and forecasts, but does not appear to factor in the psychological effects: emotionally scarred consumers are likely to spend less and save more, bringing about a kind of 'Great Depression mind-set'. It seems that the sense of vulnerability will be long lasting, in that anxiety and fear as a result of the virus could outlast the pandemic itself.

Those who are financially crippled by the crisis or who experience the loss of loved ones are also the most susceptible to enduring psychological trauma and those who already had mental health problems, such as addiction, are also at risk. They will clearly find it much harder to draw on their resilience in order to bounce back.

A Recovery Toolbox for Wellbeing in the Early Years

This most at-risk group also includes the front-line service personnel and essential workers for whom mental health disorders inflicted during this crisis could exceed the consequences of the virus itself. However, it is also evident that that even those who are not directly affected by the crisis are at risk for post-traumatic stress disorder. For example, after 9/11 it became evident that even people who were not directly exposed to trauma, but spent many hours in front of the television or looking at their smart phones, were at high risk for psychopathology, including PTSD, depression and anxiety.

So, more than ever before, we can see the need to provide the appropriate support at an individual and whole-systems level for all populations experiencing this mental trauma. We know that those who suffer from mental health disorders can be treated with therapeutic interventions and, in some cases, medication.

But we also need to emphasise the fact that there are steps that individuals can take – even while the crisis continues – that can curb its psychological toll, such as limiting exposure to television news and social media, connecting with others, developing effective thinking skills, looking after their diet and exercise regimes, practising grounding and using a range of strategies to self-regulate the nervous system.

What prompted us to write this series of books was our sense of the enormity of this whole situation, as well as our feelings of helplessness to change things and make a difference. In effect, we wanted to play the role that we believe is the duty of psychologists. We needed to feel that we could encourage others – particularly young people – to take back some level of control and achieve a sense of autonomy, and one way to do this was to create these 3 publications.

Giving psychology away has always been our joint aim. We now, more than ever, need to share what we know and empower others to make use of the evidence-based tools that work – we can no longer be precious about this. We are not suggesting we all can become therapists, but we are making the argument that, given this current crisis, it is more vital than ever that we do all become more therapeutic and learn how to use the strategies that therapists know to be effective. Most of this is common sense in our view and not rocket science. As you read, you will see how easy it can be to begin to ground yourself, to challenge negative thinking, to self-soothe, to connect and to self-regulate with Mindfulness and tools from Positive Psychology.

We both live and breathe this stuff. It comes from the heart. So, if this helps you and your children begin to take back a little bit of control and manage this ongoing level of stress and trauma then our work will have been worthwhile.

Tina Rae & Ali D'Amario
August 2020

What did primary school children say?

It feels like being trapped sometimes. Then, when we go out of the house, it's like we're free, like a bird out of its cage for the first time.

Emma age 11

My dad works in a hospital as a doctor. We can't hug him when he comes home until he takes a shower. He is at the hospital many times until night time.

Adrian age 7

Staying home has made me realize that this is the perfect time to bond with your family.

Araina age 9

If my friends are perhaps reading this, I do want to say I really miss them.

Madelynn age 11

This new virus can be pretty scary. If you're someone who's easily worried, my advice is to talk to someone you know well about how you feel. Sometimes they can reassure you.

Holly age 9

I don't get to see my friends much, or my Dad. He works for the hospital. I appreciate what essential workers are doing to keep the world safe!

Caleb age 8

One week turned into two weeks, two weeks turned into four weeks, and all of the sudden we weren't going back to school this year. This makes me really sad.

Maddie age 9

I'm annoyed because covid has made a big problem, and we can't hug friends anymore and we can't go to activities anymore.

It was really boring when we had no school work to do (during first lockdown) and when we couldn't see our friends.

The best part was having the whole school playground to ourselves (in the small keyworker group) and making a new friend (in her mixed age range keyworker bubble).

Emma age 10

I'm worried about when the other children come back to school. It's going to be different and noisy and scary.

Daniel age 10

I have Type 1 Diabetes and I'm scared that if I get Covid, I'll die.

Jake age 11

About the Authors

Dr Ali D'Amario is an educational and child psychologist working for the Xavier Catholic Education Trust. Within her role, she leads a team of 'mental health champions', trains and supervises emotional literacy support assistants, delivers training and parent workshops, as well as working with children at a group and individual level.

She trained at the University of East London under the supervision of Dr Tina Rae, who she credits for instilling her with a passion for supporting the wellbeing of others through nurture, compassion and all things kind. She is proud to be on the editorial advisory board for NurtureUK's *International Journal of Nurture in Education* (IJNE), and is co-author, with Tina Rae, of *Philosophy for Children: The man in the moon* (2014).

@AliDamarioEP

Dr Tina Rae has more thirty years' experience working with children, adults and families in both clinical and educational contexts within local authorities and specialist educational services. She currently works as a consultant educational and child psychologist in a range of SEMH and mainstream contexts and for Compass Fostering as a consultant psychologist supporting foster carers, social workers and looked-after children. From 2010 to 2016 she was an academic and professional tutor for the Doctorate in Educational and Child Psychology at the University of East London. Tina is a registered member of the Health and Care Professions Council and a full member of the British Psychological Society. She is also a member of ENSEC (European Network for Social and Emotional Competence) and a former trustee of the Nurture Group Network (NGN) now NurtureUK.

Tina is an award-winning author of more than 100 titles on topics including wellbeing, attachment, emotional literacy, behavioural problems, anger and stress management, critical incidents, Cognitive Behavioural Therapy, motivational interviewing, solution-focused brief therapy, loss and bereavement in young people, youth offending and social skills development.

Among her most recent publications are *A Toolbox of Wellbeing* (2020), *The ASD Girls' Wellbeing Toolkit: An evidence-based intervention promoting mental, physical & emotional health* (2019; Winner of the BESA Education Resources Awards 2020 Education Book of Year), *The Essential Guide to Using CBT with Children & Young People* (2018), *Identifying & Supporting Children with Sensory Processing Difficulties* (2018), *Understanding & Preventing Self-Harm in Schools* (2017), *The Essential Guide to Using Mindfulness with Children & Young People* (2017), all from Hinton House Publishers.

Tina is a regular speaker at both national and international conferences and provides training courses and supervision for school-based staff in special and mainstream contexts and educational psychology services across the UK and internationally.

tinarae@hotmail.co.uk
@DrTinarae

Introduction

The Recovery Toolbox, aimed at nurturing post-traumatic growth with children and young people, can be regarded as a must-have series of books for providing much needed practical advice and support to protect mental health and wellbeing at a time of uncertainty and fear.

A recent survey undertaken by the charity Young Minds in March 2020 revealed that the current coronavirus pandemic is having a profound effect on young people with existing mental health conditions. Although they understood the need for the measures taken in response to the virus, the report says, this did not lessen the impact. Many of those who took part in the survey reported increased anxiety, problems with sleep, panic attacks or more frequent urges to self-harm.

Professionals who work in the young people's mental health sector are continuing to provide support where they can and going to remarkable lengths to reach young people, even though face-to-face contact is now usually restricted and remote support is often challenging, according to Emma Thomas, Chief Executive of Young Minds.

> *While we recognise the huge efforts being made, we need to find ways to help those young people who have lost their support – not least because, in many cases, they have also lost many of their coping mechanisms, including contact with friends or routines that help them to manage their conditions. We also know that many young people who previously might not have needed mental health support are likely to do so in future.*
>
> *BBC News online, April 2020*

Why We Wrote this Book

It is this research and our own personal awareness of the impact of this traumatic and frightening context that has primarily prompted us to write this series of books.

We know that the impact upon all of us is significant and, for those who already have mental health issues, the ongoing sense of fear and anxiety is especially concerning. The sense of uncertainty and the transition to a new and insecure reality and ways of living will continue to impact upon all of us – adults and children alike.

The need to understand the impact of such trauma on the whole community has never been more vital. Although young people in the Young Minds survey were able to identify some of the factors that they found helpful in a time of trauma, we recognised that there will be an ongoing need for us all to develop and make use of trauma-informed approaches in the aftermath of this pandemic. Children will need to find and build upon their inner resources of resilience and adults will need to do likewise, alongside learning how to talk to children about their fears and to do so in a therapeutic way that enables them to heal and to cope in their new reality.

The increase in anxiety

Another organisation that has noticed changes as a result of coronavirus is Shout, a free 24-hour texting service for people in crisis. During the last week in March 2020, they experienced a steady increase in the number of people contacting them, peaking at more than 1,000 conversations on one day.

Around 70 per cent of their texters are under the age of 25 and in that age group they have seen a growing number of conversations about coronavirus, currently around 25 per cent of all conversations daily. Alongside that, they are seeing an increase in conversations about anxiety, while conversations about coronavirus are almost twice as likely to involve anxiety (60 per cent) as usual.

The ongoing concern

We know that our children and those who already have existing mental health issues will be finding the current lockdown experience particularly stressful and increased levels of anxiety will be the norm. However, it is probably also the case that every child will be experiencing higher levels of stress and anxiety at this time and that when they do eventually return to the school context there will be enormous emotional and psychological hurdles to overcome. The need to provide support for increased levels of anxiety and managing the transition to a 'new normal' will be ongoing.

> *Never has there been a time when knowing how to manage your own wellbeing and how to support our children in doing this has been so vital.*

The focus on Primary school children

This book therefore focuses on providing resources and strategies specifically for children aged 7 to 11 alongside advice for teachers/parents and carers as to how to support them to build resilience, self-esteem, social skills, effective thinking, manage anxiety and worries and the transition back into their primary school settings settings.

Introduction

In the COVID-19 series: briefing on schools the researchers found that some pupils' concentration or their mental and physical stamina had reduced during the initial lockdown period. Some leaders also said that pupils were fatigued, 'disconnected' from learning or struggling to stay awake and alert. Some teachers also identified a deterioration in pupils' behaviour and willingness to follow rules compared with when they first returned to school in September 2020. In some schools, leaders reported an increase in anti-social behaviour and/or aggression. These dips in behaviour were attributed in some cases to having experienced domestic violence, trauma and mental health issues at home while the schools were closed to most children.

In terms of mental well-being, leaders across several schools reported increased cases of pupils self-harming, mainly over the period when schools were closed to most pupils. Some also noted that more pupils were suffering from eating disorders, many of whom had not previously been identified as vulnerable. A significant concern is that these behaviours were now more prevalent in Primary aged pupils and some younger pupils in primary schools were also experiencing increased attachment to their parents or home as a result of being at home for so long.

Some children had also lost elements of independence, for example forgetting how to use a knife and fork. Headteachers also noted that some pupils were struggling to interact with their peers due to prolonged isolation and needed to relearn how to maintain friendships. This was further compounded by class or year-group bubble restrictions, which meant that pupils could not socialise as they typically would.

It is the findings from this research and our own personal awareness of the impact of this traumatic and frightening context that has primarily prompted us to write this series of books. It is clearly evident that many of our children at this stage in their education will have been significantly affected by the experiences of Lockdowns and transitioning back into schools which now look and feel very different.

We know that the impact upon all of us is significant and, for those who already have mental health issues, the ongoing sense of fear and anxiety is especially concerning. The sense of uncertainty and the transition to a new and insecure reality and ways of living will continue to impact on all of us – adults and children alike.

The need to understand the impact of such trauma on the whole community has never been more vital. Although many primary school children have been able to to identify some of the things that they found helpful in a time of trauma, we recognise that there will be an ongoing need for us all to develop and make use of trauma-informed approaches in the aftermath of this pandemic.

As stated previously, Children will need to find and build upon their inner resources of resilience and adults will need to do likewise, as well as learning how to talk to their children about their fears in a therapeutic way that enables them to heal and to cope in their new reality. Understanding emotional and psychological trauma and the ways in which we can help children (and ourselves) to heal and engage in post-traumatic growth is clearly now an essential objective for us all.

What is Emotional & Psychological Trauma?

Emotional and psychological trauma is the result of **extraordinarily stressful events** that shatter our sense of security, making us feel helpless in a dangerous world. Psychological trauma can leave us struggling with upsetting emotions, memories and anxiety that does not seem to go away. It can also leave us feeling numb, disconnected and unable to trust other people.

Traumatic experiences often involve a threat to life or safety, but any situation that leaves us feeling overwhelmed and isolated can result in trauma, even if it does not involve physical harm. It is not the objective circumstances that determine whether an event is traumatic, but our subjective emotional experience of the event. The more frightened and helpless we feel, the more likely we are to be traumatised. Repeatedly viewing traumatic images can overwhelm our nervous system and create traumatic stress. This is certainly true in terms of access to social media and news reporting regarding the current pandemic. We know that the increase in anxiety for many of us is directly linked to continual exposure to such material. However, whatever the cause of our trauma, and whether it happened years ago or yesterday, we can make healing changes and move forwards – even flourishing in the post-traumatic growth period that ensues.

Protecting the Mental Health of Children after Trauma

The effects of traumatic experiences on children are sobering, but not all children are affected in the same way, or to the same degree. Children and families possess competencies, psychological resources and resilience (often even in the face of significant trauma) that can protect them from long-term harm. Teaching children the skills of resilience and providing them with opportunities to bounce back and renew themselves in the face of adversity is a precious gift.

- **Be there**. Research on resilience in children demonstrates that an essential protective factor is the reliable presence of a positive, caring and protective parent, caregiver, or significant other (such as a teacher), who can help shield children against adverse experiences (Sroufe *et al.*, 2005).

Introduction

- **Support them to challenge underlying beliefs & thoughts.** Negative and irrational beliefs and thoughts, such as, 'If I don't look perfect, no one will like me', or 'I can't cope with difficult or scary situations,' are significant factors in generating anxiety. Model and communicate effective ways to question and challenge anxiety-provoking thoughts and beliefs.

- **Support them to accept uncertainty.** Uncertainty is one thing that people worry about a lot because of the potential for negative outcomes. As it is impossible to eliminate uncertainty, you can assist children to be more accepting of uncertainty and ambiguity.

- **Be a role model.** If you can manage your own anxiety, children will see that it can be managed and incorporate your strategies into their own behaviours. Teaching parents to manage their own anxiety has been shown to be helpful in reducing their children's anxiety.

- **Be patient.** Sometimes the behaviours of anxious children may seem unreasonable to others. It is important to remember that an anxious child who cries or avoids situations is, in fact, responding instinctively to a perceived threat. Changing avoidant behaviours takes time and persistence.

- **Balance reassurance with new ideas.** When a child comes to you with something they are worried about, listen and understand what is happening. Explore with them what they could do to manage their fears.

- **Show children some simple relaxation techniques.** Deep breathing, progressive muscle relaxation and meditation can be helpful as a way of learning how to better manage physical anxiety symptoms. Generally, these techniques are only effective if practised consistently over several weeks

- **Encourage plenty of physical exercise and appropriate sleep.** When people are well-rested and relaxed, they will be in a better mental state to handle fears or worries.

- **Moderate the consumption of products high in sugar.** High sugar products increase levels of anxiety, because they cause energy levels to spike and then crash. This leaves a person feeling drained and less able to deal with negative thoughts.

- **Make time for things that the child enjoys and finds relaxing.** These could be simple things, such as playing or listening to music, reading books or going for walks.

- **Help them to face the things or situations they fear.** Learning to face their fears and reduce avoidance of feared objects and situations, is one of the most challenging parts of overcoming anxiety. Facing fears usually works best if it is undertaken gradually, a step at a time.

- **Encourage help-seeking when needed.** Make sure that children know there are people who can help if they find that they cannot handle a problem on their own. Knowing that they can call on others for support, if needed, will make them feel less anxious about what might happen in the future.

The need to be resilient yourself

We know that unregulated and stressed adults cannot effectively support and help children who are also unregulated and stressed. It is impossible.

We also know that the direct carers of children are most effective in helping them develop self-regulation. They can provide activities that support regulation and are also the most immediate role models for children. The emotional tone of a school or children's home is dramatically affected by the capacity of adults to regulate themselves. If adults respond to children's distress in a calm but engaged way, they demonstrate an alternative way of managing stress. When adults respond to difficulties by becoming dysregulated, they replicate the damaging environments that characterised children's earlier experiences.

Kolk (2003) described trauma as 'speechless terror' and traumatised children may be slow to develop speech or may struggle to find words to describe their trauma or their feelings. Trauma may also affect the capacity to process verbal information. Traumatised children can struggle to follow complex directions and may experience auditory selectivity, so that only part of a verbal communication is heard. Adults often interpret failure to obey directions or to respond to questions as wilful defiance and react punitively, rather than modifying their own communication to match the children's needs. So, once again, we need to be careful to ensure that our responses and the systems we put in place, both in the home and in school, ensure these factors are considered. We must respond appropriately to children and young people who have experienced trauma and who are currently living through the traumatic times of this pandemic. We need to create safety routines first and to also change our own expectations and behaviours.

To achieve this, we need to ensure that we know how to engage in effective self-care and how to manage our own stress and anxiety, whilst simultaneously understanding the need to respond in a truly trauma-informed way. This has never been more important when we know that children are all experiencing such a stressful social and educational context (See Appendix 5, 'Trauma Recovery Self-Care Tips').

The need to provide feelings of safety at home & in school

Looking at the sensory environments where children live and learn can help to create feelings of safety. Our brains develop by recognising novel stimuli that may potentially indicate danger, but, in order to manage the sensory bombardment we all experience, we quickly tune out familiar stimuli. Eventually we just do not notice sensory signals that are familiar to us, but which may be very frightening or arousing to children who are hyper-vigilant. Working alongside children, we may identify and eliminate sensory triggers that affect them negatively and build in sensory cues that are soothing or appropriately stimulating.

At times children's behaviour is considered difficult or controlling, for example, needing a light on throughout the night or being unable to sleep without music to fill the unbearable silence, but these may be attempts to feel safe. Helping children create a sensory environment that manages their traumatic responses and provides new experiences that evoke safety, allows them a sense of control over their distress that can build strength and resilience.

Traumatised children find change exceedingly difficult. Disruption of routines, even for a positive reason, can evoke panic in children. Clear stable routines are very comforting to children, particularly at times involving transition from one state to another, such as shifting from sleeping to wakefulness, or moving from one place to another, such as from home to school. Where change is anticipated it is important to explain the reasons and rehearse with children what will be different and how they will be supported. When unexpected disruption arises, adults should be alert to the likely impact on children and proactively intervene to help them remain calm.

This is not always easy in the context of a busy school and very often the level of nurture and additional consideration may cause difficulties for some adults who do not have the capacity to manage on a day to day basis. Therefore, additional training and support may well be needed. This will be particularly important when transitioning children and young people back into the school communities after the current pandemic. There will be many children who will find this traumatic and have countless questions, concerns and fears about this whole process.

The need for additional training & support

We know that understanding the impact of trauma requires both cognitive and emotional learning. This is best accomplished by linking information about trauma with practitioners' own experience of caring for or educating traumatised children. Rather than employing a simple didactic approach, it should include reflective space for participants to consider their own attachment and trauma histories, as well as those of the children they care for.

Golding (2013), for example, has created a training resource for foster carers and adoptive parents incorporating concepts from attachment and trauma theory with practice-based discussion. PACE, a parenting attitude characterised by **p**layfulness, **a**cceptance, **c**uriosity and **e**mpathy, is explored in depth and carers are encouraged to try this out between sessions. She also introduces the concept of 'mind-mindedness' to help carers understand the internal worlds of children and fill developmental gaps created by an early failure of attuned and mind-mindful parenting. As well as increasing carers' knowledge, the course aims to decrease their stress and thus contributes to the stability of placements.

Engaging with traumatised children in an open and connected way is itself stressful and difficult and there is always a risk that practitioners and carers will experience vicarious trauma. 'Blocked care' (Hughes & Baylin, 2013) is a concept that describes the neurological impact on adults of caring for children who are unable to engage in reciprocal relationships. Hughes and Baylin describe 'brain-based' parenting as a way of investing in reflective support that can avert dangers to both children and those who care for or educate them.

Knowledge and understanding of brain-based nurturing should now become a key element in school strategies and new ways of parenting if we are to successfully meet the needs of our children and young people as they recover from the trauma of this pandemic.

It is also now essential that school leaders provide mental health training for all staff to ensure that there is a coherent and evidence-based approach to meeting the increasingly complex needs of the school population. This is not an easy task, given current financial and logistical constraints, but there are many useful resources available that are cost effective and can provide staff with a knowledge base and sense of confidence in their ability to develop their skills in responding to, and working more therapeutically with, children and young people. The role of the mental health leads in schools will be key here in leading the development of appropriate training and making use of available evidence-based training resources, such as *The Wellbeing Toolkit for Mental Health Leads* (Rae et al., 2020).

Communicating authentically is key

Children and young people need to feel validated, heard and safe and adults need more than ever to develop the skills of authentic listening and the ability to emotion coach children through the feelings and behaviours they will experience on a daily basis. These are essential skills and the process of using emotion coaching needs to permeate our thinking and responses, both as parents and carers (See Appendix 4, 'Emotion Coaching Information').

To help a child recover from trauma, it is important for adults to communicate openly. They need to let them know that it is normal to feel scared or upset, and to remember that children may also look to them for cues on how they should respond to trauma; therefore letting them see how we are dealing with our own symptoms in a positive way is vital.

How Children React to Emotional & Psychological Trauma

- **Regression.** Many children need to return to an earlier stage where they felt safer. Younger children may wet the bed or want a bottle; older children may fear being alone. It is important to be understanding, patient and comforting if our child responds in this way.

- **Thinking the event is their fault.** Children younger than 8 years of age tend to think that if something goes wrong, it must be their fault. Be sure that the child understands that they did not cause the event.

- **Sleep disorders.** Some children have difficulty falling asleep; others wake frequently or have troubling dreams. Giving a younger child a stuffed animal, soft blanket, or flashlight to take to bed can be helpful, alongside spending extra time together in the evening, doing quiet activities or reading. Patience is key here. It may take a while before a child can sleep through the night again.

- **Feeling helpless.** Being active in a campaign to prevent an event from happening again, writing thank-you letters to people who have helped, and caring for others can bring a sense of hope and control to everyone in the family.

To summarise the key points, the things we know about trauma:

- Children in care are likely to have experienced trauma, but not all children who have adverse experiences will be traumatised. Every child is unique and their responses to the same adversity will differ.

- Trauma can affect brain development. Many traumatised children function at an earlier developmental level than their chronological age suggests.

- Traumatised children may struggle to develop regulatory skills needed for learning and social relationships.

- Some children react powerfully to sensory triggers related to their trauma by becoming hyper-aroused or dissociating. These reactions often occur below the level of conscious awareness.

- If adults involved with traumatised children are unable to manage their own emotions, this can escalate children's distress.

- Effective help requires intervention that is congruent with neuroscience, developmentally relevant and relational.

- The key adults in helping children recover from trauma are their carers and teachers. They require relevant support and training to be most helpful to traumatised children.

- Post-traumatic growth and resilience is possible. Traumatised children need hope and adults involved with them must believe in a positive future for them.

Using the Recovery Toolbox

If we think about looking after our bodies and keeping fit and well it is easy to see how we also need to look after what is happening in our heads – how we think, feel and react to what happens to us in life.

Having good mental health means that we are generally able to think, feel and react in ways that make us able to connect with other people and lead a healthy and generally happy life. Not being able to manage our emotional, psychological and social wellbeing can feel just as bad as a physical illness, or even worse.

Introduction

We have written this book with the intention of providing children and young people and their carers/teachers easy to understand and use tools and strategies to foster good mental health and to build the resilience needed to move on from trauma – including that of having to live with the continual fear of the current coronavirus pandemic.

All the activities are self-explanatory and straightforward. We have included additional detail in the appendices to explain in more detail some key tools, such as Mindfulness or strategies from Cognitive Behavioural Therapy (CBT) where we think this might be needed.

However, the idea here is to make this all accessible to the non-specialist. We want people to be able to pick up this book and feel safe in making use of the ideas and know that this is all evidence-based and has been tried and tested with children and young people over many years. This is *not* a therapeutic handbook and certainly does not replace the role of the specialist therapeutic professional. This is a resource for the non-specialist who is seeking to better understand mental health issues and protective factors and who needs to support and nurture our anxious children and young people at a time of real crisis in both education and in the social context.

A final note of caution

If the psychological trauma symptoms *do not* ease up – or if they become even worse – and the individual finds that they are unable to move on from the event for a prolonged period of time, they may be experiencing post-traumatic stress disorder. While emotional trauma is a normal response to a disturbing event, it becomes PTSD when our nervous system gets 'stuck' and we remain in psychological shock, unable to make sense of what happened or process our emotions.

Working through trauma can be scary, painful, and potentially re-traumatising, so this healing work is best undertaken with the help of an experienced trauma specialist.

To seek additional help of this nature for a child (or an adult) it is clearly essential in the first instance to discuss with the GP and then to seek an appropriate referral. A list of specialist agencies and charities are included in the appendices to this book, which may also be helpful should you need to seek additional support.

1 Self-Regulation Activities

Self-regulation is the ability to understand and control your behaviour and your emotional reactions. This includes being able to calm yourself down when experiencing big emotions, such as anxiety, anger or excitement. Self-regulation skills also allow us to focus on the task at hand, and respond with socially appropriate behaviour, rather than showing how we might really feel. We develop these skills as we grow and our brains develop; hence, while a 2-year-old might throw themselves on the floor in the supermarket when they are bored, an older child or adult may respond differently to the same feelings. Self-regulation skills are important because they help children to control their impulses, maintain relationships with other children during play, and manage their stress levels. Through this self-regulation, they are able to feel safe, content, and able to learn.

Self-regulation skills start to develop in infancy. When children have experienced co-regulation through consistent, sensitive relationships, they begin to learn how to manage their own emotions. Neuroscientific research suggests that these relationships help to develop the links between the emotional limbic brain and the cerebral cortex, allowing children to be better able to rationalise, reason, empathise and problem-solve. However, the cerebral cortex is not thought to be fully developed until the mid-twenties, and therefore children, adolescents and even adults need support with self-regulation at times. Due to their brain development, it is crucial to support a child to regulate their emotions before trying to reason with them.

Some calming techniques to teach young children to help them self-regulate include:

- Mindfulness
- Visualisation
- Grounding
- Sensory activities
- Controlled breathing

These techniques have been incorporated into the activities in this section, along with activities designed to help your children to identify their emotions. Research shows that labelling emotions can help to reduce the intensity of the emotion (Torre & Lieberman, 2018), and therefore teaching this skill is integral in allowing children to start to manage their own emotions.

Activity 1.1
Square Breathing

When you find yourself feeling overwhelmed by your emotions, this exercise can help to distract your mind and slow down your breathing to calm the body. No matter where you are, if you look around you, you should be able to find something square or rectangular (e.g., a window, a whiteboard, a table, a page of a book, an exam paper, a picture – the list is endless!). Focus on that square and trace it with your eyes whilst you do the following exercise. Repeat until you can feel your body start to relax and unwind.

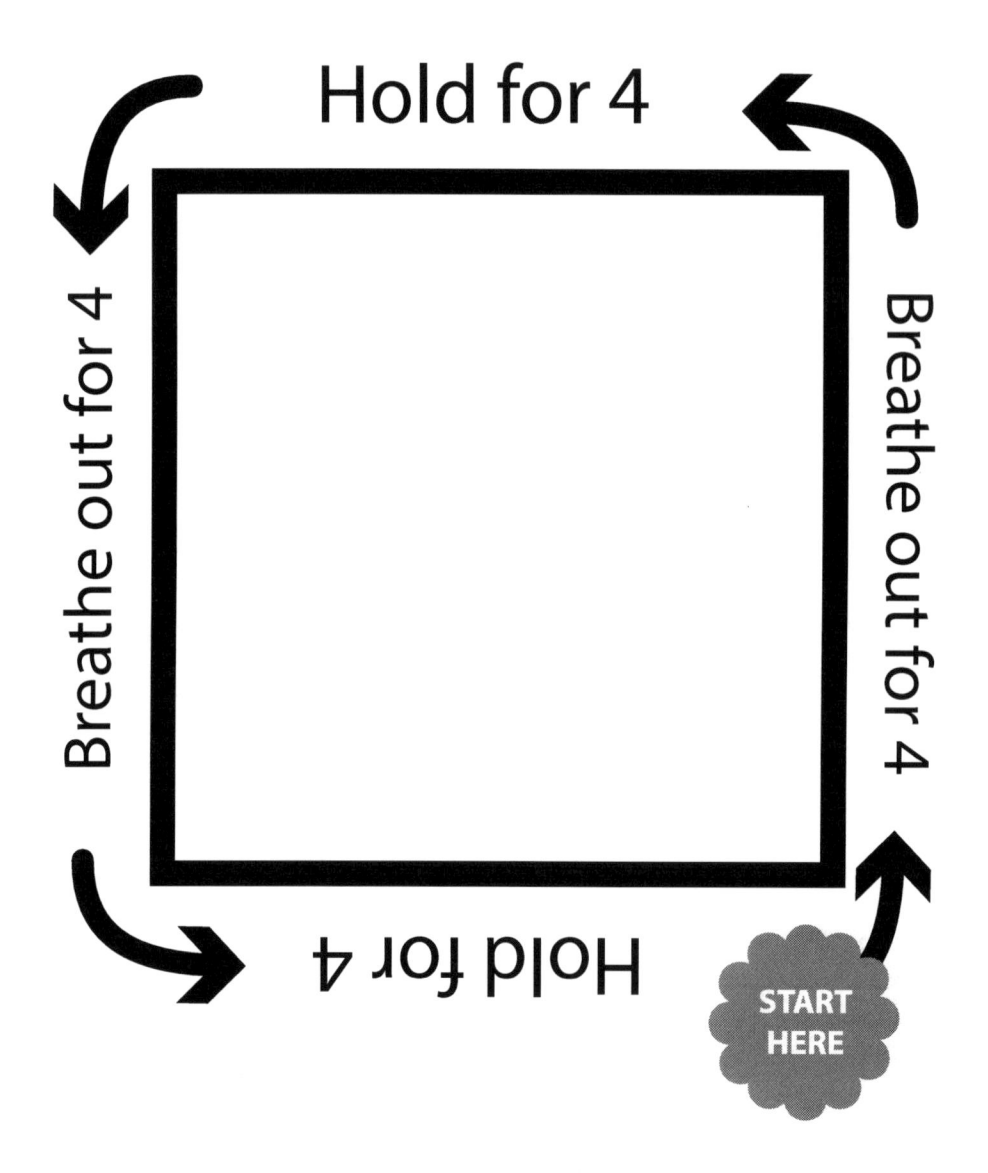

```
            Hold for 4
    ┌─────────────────────┐
    │                     │
Breathe                Breathe
out for 4              out for 4
    │                     │
    └─────────────────────┘
            Hold for 4
                    START HERE
```

How did it make you feel afterwards?

When might this technique be useful?

Activity 1.2
Hand Breathing

Hand breathing is a technique that can be used very subtly anywhere, and at any time, to regulate the breathing and calm the nervous system. Trace up and down your fingers as shown below, breathing in for 4 seconds as you trace up, and then out for 4 seconds as you trace down. Repeat this across both hands several times until you feel calm.

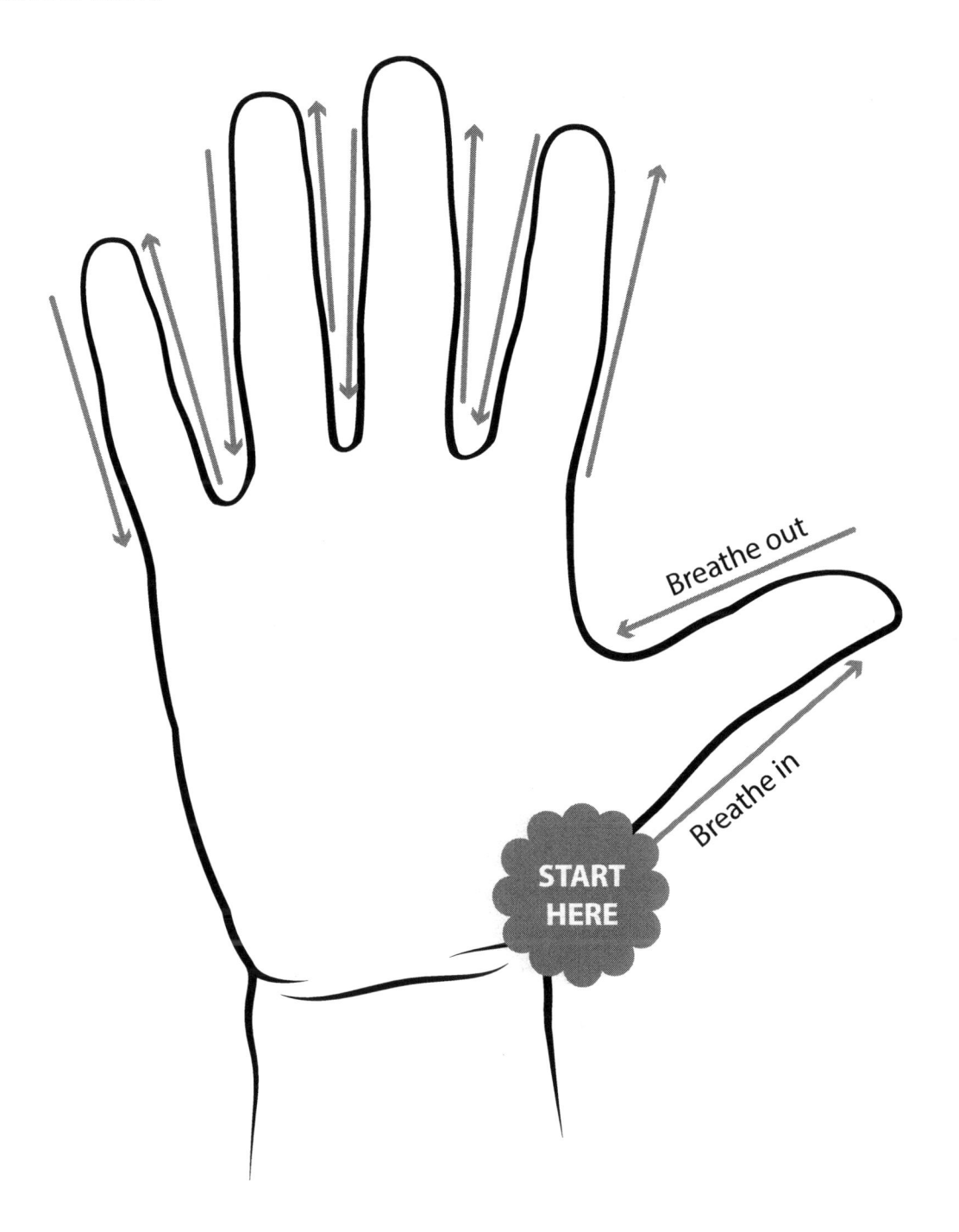

Breathe out

Breathe in

START HERE

Activity 1.3
Anger Iceberg

Think of a time when you felt really angry. What happened and how did it make you feel?

_____

_____

_____

Often, when we feel anger, there are actually lots of other emotions below the surface. Identifying these can help us to manage our emotions better.

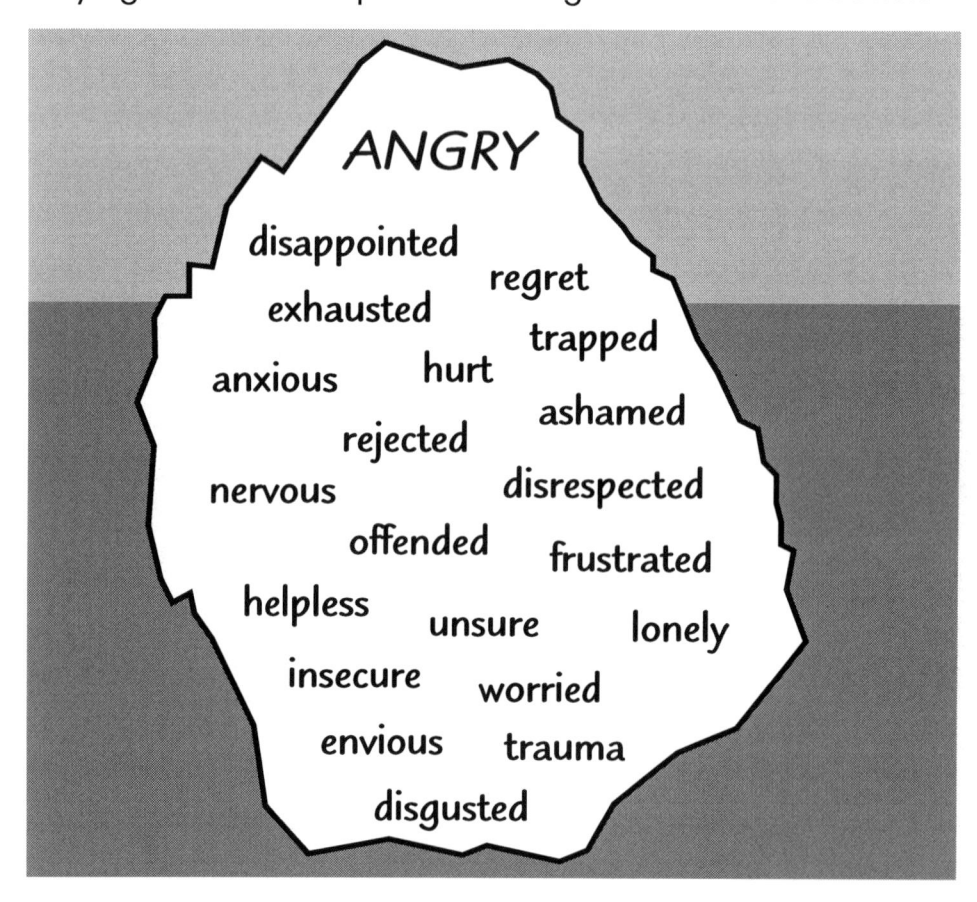

ANGRY

disappointed, regret, exhausted, trapped, anxious, hurt, ashamed, rejected, nervous, disrespected, offended, frustrated, helpless, unsure, lonely, insecure, worried, envious, trauma, disgusted

Can you identify any other emotions that could have been under the surface in the incident that you describe above?

_____

_____

Activity 1.4
Grounding the Senses

Focusing on the present moment allows us to stop worrying about the future or dwelling on the past. As a result, it can be a lovely way to help us to feel calmer and take a break from our big uncomfortable emotions, such as anxiety, anger and sadness.

Wherever you are, focus on what you can sense around you by trying to find:

Five things that you can see . . .

1 _____
2 _____
3 _____
4 _____
5 _____

Four things that you can hear . . .

1 _____
2 _____
3 _____
4 _____

Three things that you can touch . . .

1 _____
2 _____
3 _____

Two things that you can smell . . .

1 _____
2 _____

One thing you can taste . . .

1 _____

Then take **one** deep breath.

Activity 1.5
Mindful Eating

Mindfulness does not always have to mean sitting quietly and meditating; you can also undertake daily activities in a mindful way (see Appendix 2, 'Mindfulness Information'). Mindful eating involves focusing the senses on the present moment and purposefully noticing how the food looks, smells, feels, tastes – and even how it sounds! You can try this with any food, but Maltesers or raisins are commonly used for this activity.

How does it look? What do you notice about the colour, shape and surface texture?

_____
_____

How does it smell?

_____
_____

If you are using a raisin, put it close to your ear and squish it between your fingers, what do you hear?

_____
_____

How does it feel between your fingers?

_____
_____

Pop it in your mouth and notice how it feels against your tongue.

_____

What can you taste? Does it taste different at the front and back of your mouth?

_____

Reflection

What did you notice about the food that you had never noticed previously?

How do you feel afterwards?

Activity 1.6
Mindful Clapping

Clap your hands together and then hold them apart as if you are holding an invisible football. Keep your hands in position for as long as you can still 'feel the clap' in your hands.

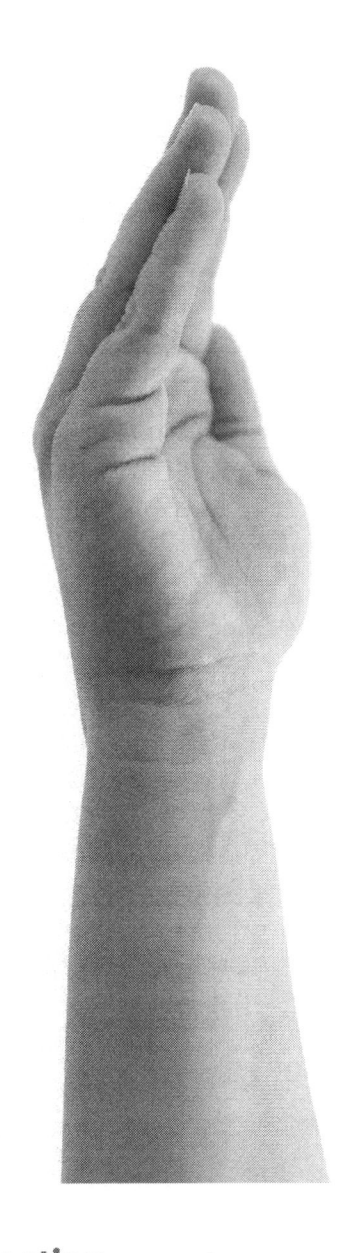

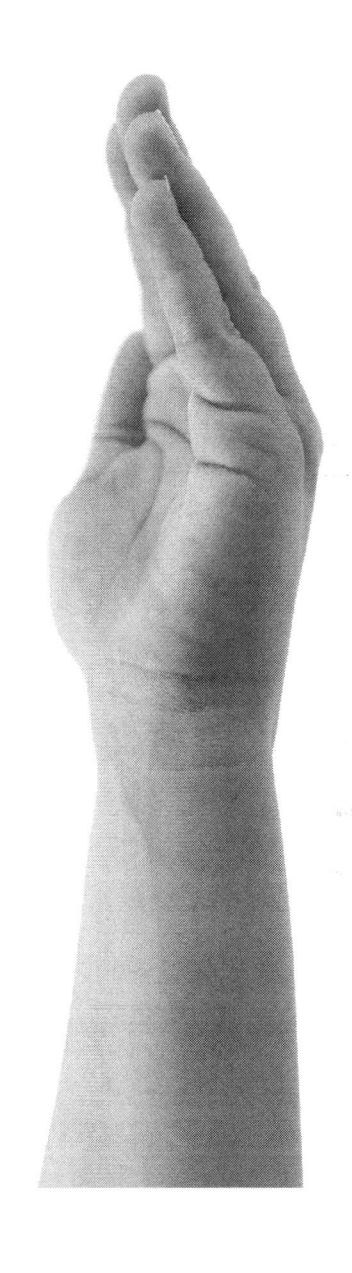

Reflection

How do you feel afterwards?

When might you use this to ground yourself and take your mind away from an uncomfortable thought or feeling?

Activity 1.7
Visualisation

Use this script to help your child to relax and focus their mind on something positive.

Find a comfortable position. This could be sitting on a chair with your feet on the floor and hands on your lap, or you may be happier lying on the floor. Once you are settled, close your eyes and take a nice deep breath, in through your nose, and then out through your mouth. Focus for a moment on your breath, feeling your tummy rise as you breathe in and fall as you slowly breathe out.

Imagine that it's a beautiful sunny day and you are lying on a beach next to the crystal-clear turquoise ocean. Your body sinks into the warm sand, which is shaped perfectly around you, making you feel safe and cosy. In the distance, you can hear the sound of the waves lapping gently and you can smell the fresh aroma of flowers in the air from the beautiful gardens behind you. Your body feels completely relaxed and you feel a deep sense of contentment, knowing that you are safe, you are happy, and you are loved.

Activity 1.8
Body Scanning Script

This script can be a really helpful tool to support children in relaxing before going to sleep.

Lie down on your back, or sit comfortably in a chair with your feet on the floor and your hands in your lap. Once you feel settled and comfortable, slowly close your eyes and take a nice deep breath, in through your nose and out through your mouth. Notice how with every breath you feel more and more relaxed.

We are going to take the time to focus on each part of your body to help you to relax. Start with your feet: focus on relaxing them and allow them to fall to the side. Notice any tension you might feel in your ankle and allow it to slowly melt away. Now move your attention to your lower legs and knees. Focus on any tightness in your muscles, tensing them gently and then relaxing them completely. Move your attention up to your upper legs, noticing the heaviness of your hands on your thighs and the feeling of material against your skin. Now focus on your tummy. Notice it moving when you breathe, rising and falling again, like waves on the ocean. If you notice any tight, worried feelings in your tummy, take a deep breath and, as you exhale, feel your tummy relax and the feelings dissolve. Next, bring your attention to your chest and shoulders. Notice any tension in your shoulders and gently relax them down away from your neck. Turn your attention to your hands. Whatever you feel against your skin, soften your touch and lighten your hands, imagining that they are resting softly on a cloud. Allow your arms to hang loosely and move your attention up to your face. Soften your expression, feeling it melt away as you let every muscle in your face relax.

Take a few moments to notice how relaxed you feel as you continue to focus on taking deep breaths, in and out.

Activity 1.9
Calming Positions

Hand on heart

Sit on the floor with your legs crossed and your back straight. Relax your neck and shoulders, and place one hand on your heart and one on your tummy. Take 10 deep breaths in through the nose and out through the mouth.

FOFBOC

Sit comfortably with your feet on the floor and bottom on the chair (FOFBOC). As you sit, notice that you feel safe and supported. Bring awareness to the places in your body where you can feel pressure. Imagine that you can draw energy from the ground through your feet. Take 10 deep breaths to help you to feel grounded and at peace.

Sweet dreams

Close your eyes and, with your mouth closed, imagine that you are sucking on a delicious sweet. Take 10 deep breaths to help you to feel soothed and comforted.

Activity 1.10
Regulate the Senses

Try some of these sensory activities to help to regulate and calm your senses:

- Jog around the playground
- Bounce a ball
- Blow some bubbles
- Listen to music
- Go climbing
- Hum or sing
- Hang upside down
- Swing slowly
- Press your shoulder against something
- Wrap up in a blanket
- Work with lavender-scented playdough
- Sit in a rocking chair
- Put a weighted blanket over your body

2 Resilience-Building Activities

Resilience is defined as 'the process of adapting well in the face of adversity' (American Psychological Association, 2012), and is sometimes referred to as our ability to 'bounce back' from adversity. It is important to note there are not 'resilient children' and 'less-resilient children'; resilience refers to the interaction between the particular situation and the person experiencing that situation. Another essential factor is the adversity, since we cannot respond in a resilient way if we are protected from all challenges and negative experiences. Children are often quoted as being naturally resilient, but research into adverse childhood experiences and the impact that they have, suggests otherwise. Rather, it may be that children are just less able to process and demonstrate the negative emotions that they feel until later in life.

The likelihood of being able to respond with resilience can be thought of as being somewhat dependent upon the relative weight of risk factors and protective factors. Risk factors include family conflict, abuse or neglect, experiencing trauma, and living in poverty. Conversely, the Young Minds Interactive Resilience Framework provides a useful way for us to understand the factors that may help to protect the child from adversity and make it more likely that they will 'bounce back'. These include.

- Promoting a sense of belonging
- Maintaining a web of positive relationships
- Predicting good experiences and instilling a sense of hope
- Highlighting achievements
- Promoting bravery
- Helping children to problem-solve
- Thinking positively
- Being able to understand their own and others' feelings

All of these factors are things that can be promoted for any child and we hope that the activities within this chapter will help you to harness and develop these.

Activity 2.1
Positive Diary

What have been the best three things that happened today?

1. _____
2. _____
3. _____

Which three people were you grateful to know today:

1. _____
2. _____
3. _____

What are you most proud of today?

_____
_____

What did you do today that was kind?

_____
_____

Rate the day on the emoji scale!

Activity 2.2
Times that I Have Been Brave

Bravery happens when you feel scared about something, but find the strength to do it anyway. Bravery may appear on the outside to be confident and strong, but it often feels frightening at the time, and that is what makes it something to be very proud of.

Think of a few times when you have been brave and write them below:

_____
_____
_____
_____
_____
_____
_____
_____
_____
_____

How did you feel before?

_____
_____
_____

How did you feel afterwards?

_____
_____
_____

Activity 2.3
My Coping Strategies

Think of a time when you went through something that was difficult. Write your example below:

_____
_____
_____
_____
_____
_____

Now consider the coping strategies that you used to bounce back from it (e.g., talking to others, asking for help, etc.).

What did you do that made you feel better?

_____
_____
_____
_____
_____
_____

Below is a list of coping strategies. Circle the ones that you have used before.

Mindfulness   Talking to a friend   Listening to music

Exercise   Talking to my family   Yoga

Breathing techniques   Talking to an adult at school   Drawing

Are there any others that you think could help you in the future?

_____

Activity 2.4
Who Can You Talk To?

Talking to others can really help us to see our problems more clearly and reduce our worried feelings.

Who do you have to talk to? Draw them in the box below.

Label each person with the traits that they have that make them a good person to talk to.

For example: 'good at listening', 'can keep a secret', and so on.

Activity 2.5
Self-Care Checklist

Below are some things that you can do to look after yourself and keep yourself mentally healthy each day. Tick the ones that you already do.

- Eat fruit and vegetables
- Sleep for 10 to 11 hours per night
- Exercise each day
- Spend time reflecting on the positives about my day
- Do something kind for someone else
- Reflect on the things that I am grateful for
- Do something that I love doing
- Get some fresh air
- Spend time with people I love
- Practice Mindfulness
- Listen to music
- Play
- Join a club
- Learn something new

Circle at least one that you don't currently do, but would like to.

Think about how you will fit it into your day.

Activity 2.6
My Box of Things to Look Forward To

Over recent times, there have been lots of changes in our lives that have meant we are currently unable to do some of the things that we used to enjoy. Instilling a sense of hope is important for building resilience.

Spend some time thinking about things that you miss and are looking forward to doing in the future. Write them down on small pieces of paper and keep them all safe in a box, ready to open and enjoy when you are able to.

Activity 2.7
Friendly Talk for Building Resilience

When you keep experiencing the same problem, find someone else who copes with it! Talk through their strategies and steps to success!

Answer the following QUESTIONS:

- What is this problem?
  _____
  _____

- Who has successfully coped with this problem?
  _____
  _____

- How do they do this?
  _____
  _____

- When can I discuss their plan?
  _____
  _____

- What will my own plan then look like and when will I try it out?
  _____
  _____

- How will I reward myself for being successful?
  _____
  _____

Activity 2.8
Bin It!

Bin that bad habit! Use SMALL STEPS

Write down all your 'bad' habits in the box below – put them in order, with the easiest to stop at the bottom and hardest at the top.

- Pick one HABIT to dump

- Record your SMALL STEPS to SUCCESS in this box

- How will you keep calm? What is your coping self-talk?

- Who else can help or support you and how?

Have a go! Reward yourself and don't give up!

Go for it!

Activity 2.9
Positive Traits

Look at the table and put a tick against those positive traits that you feel you have.

Which can you build on and use now and in the future?

Which help you the most to stay positive and keep trying hard to reach your goals?

Kind		Insightful		Sensitive	
Intelligent		Funny		Organised	
Hardworking		Patient		Selfless	
Loyal		Realistic		Practical	
Attractive		Honest		Mature	
Down-to-earth		Generous		Focused	
Goofy		Modest		Courteous	
Creative		Serious		Grateful	
Accepting		Independent		Open-minded	
Strong		Trusting		Positive	
Friendly		Resilient		Responsible	
Flexible		Cheerful		Cooperative	
Nurturing		Self-directed		Frugal	
Thoughtful		Reliable		Tolerant	
Confident		Relaxed		Innovative	
Optimistic		Listener		Balanced	
Respectful		Brave		Motivated	
Determined		Decisive		Humble	
Skilled		Enthusiastic			
Helpful		Forgiving			

Activity 2.10
True Grit!

Assess your perseverance and ability to see things through! Developing 'true grit' will help you to cope with changes and transitions, now and beyond!

Rate yourself like this:
- 1 = not true of me
- 5 = sometimes true of me
- 10 = always true of me

1 I keep the same interests for a long time.

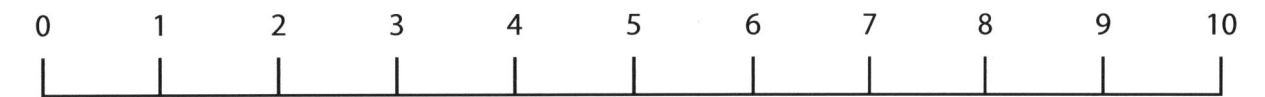

0 1 2 3 4 5 6 7 8 9 10

2 I do not lose interest in something very easily.

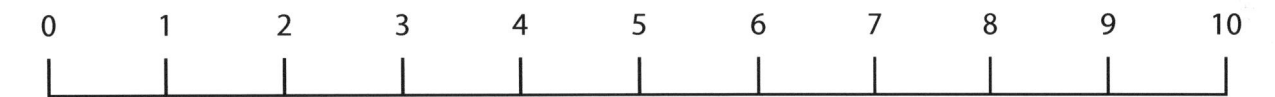

0 1 2 3 4 5 6 7 8 9 10

3 I can set goals and stick with the plan to achieve them.

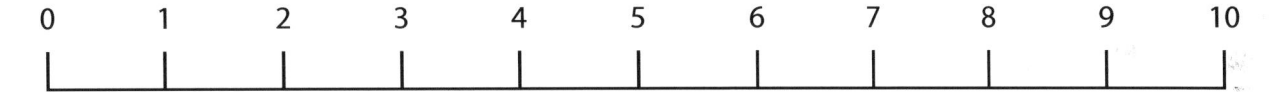

0 1 2 3 4 5 6 7 8 9 10

4 New ideas do not distract me from my goals.

0 1 2 3 4 5 6 7 8 9 10

5 I often achieve goals that took me a long time.

0 1 2 3 4 5 6 7 8 9 10

Page 1 of 2

Activity 2.10
True Grit!

6 I have overcome setbacks to meet a challenge.

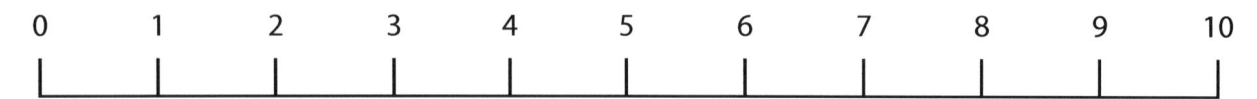

0   1   2   3   4   5   6   7   8   9   10

7 I finish whatever I begin.

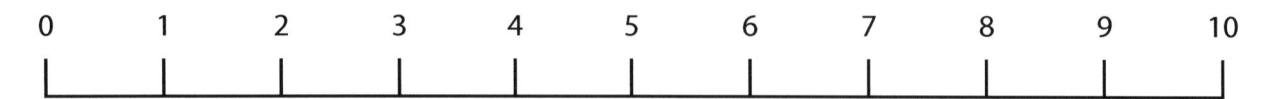

0   1   2   3   4   5   6   7   8   9   10

8 Setbacks don't put me off.

0   1   2   3   4   5   6   7   8   9   10

9 I am a hard worker.

0   1   2   3   4   5   6   7   8   9   10

10 I am a careful and thoughtful worker.

0   1   2   3   4   5   6   7   8   9   10

3 Self-Esteem & Social Skills Activities

Self-Esteem

Self-esteem is a term used to reflect a person's overall emotional evaluation of their own worth. According to educational psychologist, Michele Borba (2003), rather than being a unitary concept, self-esteem can be thought of as having five sequential components, or 'building blocks'. These are as follows:

- **Security**. This refers to feelings of safety and assuredness. The ability to trust and rely on others and to feel secure within appropriate boundaries.

- **Selfhood**. This refers to having a realistic and accurate image of who you are and what makes you an individual.

- **Affiliation**. This refers to having a sense of belonging and feeling respected, appreciated and accepted by others, particularly within the relationships that are most important to you.

- **Mission**. Refers to feeling motivated and having a sense of purpose.

- **Competence**. Refers to having a sense of achievement and success. It also involves being able to identify strengths and feel that these are valued and important, as well as accepting areas of relative weakness.

Using this description, it is clear to see that the pandemic may have impacted children's self-esteem. The message to 'stay home' and 'social distance' may have made children feel less safe, while many of their social and family relationships may have been temporarily lost; and with less immediate face-to-face feedback from school staff, many may have felt less competent and motivated.

Social Skills

Social skills

The disease control measures implemented during the pandemic have meant that interactions that children and adolescents have had with family and friends outside of the home have often been through virtual means. Whilst this has provided a valuable way for connections to be maintained, the social skills needed for virtual communication varies hugely from the social skills needed in face-to-face contact. For example, virtual communication provides fewer social cues such as body language and proximity, and relies more heavily upon good conversational and turn-taking skills. For children, much of their social interactions revolve around play, and when this is removed, the demands change which may have been challenging for many children.

These resources have been designed to support children in re-building their self-esteem, and developing their social skills in preparation for the return to school and beyond.

Activity 3.1
All About Me

Name _____ Age _____

In three words I would describe myself as . . .
_____
_____
_____

I am at my happiest when . . .
_____
_____
_____

My biggest hope for the future is . . .
_____
_____
_____

The things that help me learn most are . . .
_____
_____
_____

A very important thing that I would like you to know about me is . . .
_____
_____
_____

This page may be photocopied for instructional use only.
A Recovery Toolbox for Wellbeing for Primary-Aged Children © Tina Rae & Ali D'Amario 2021

Activity 3.2
Confidence Boosters

This is a game for two players or more. First cut out the cards below and put them in a pile where everyone can reach them.

Rules: Take turns to turn over a card and answer the question.

What are you most proud of?	What is your favourite thing about you?	What makes you unique?
When are you at your happiest?	What have you learnt about yourself this year?	When have you shown bravery?
What is the kindest thing that you have ever done?	What was the best thing that has ever happened to you?	Who appreciates you and why?
What is the nicest compliment that you have ever received?	What is your biggest talent?	How would your friend describe you?
What are you most grateful for?	Who are you grateful to?	What do you love about your life?

Activity 3.3
My Amazing Body

Read and complete the sentences below.

I am grateful for my wonderful body.

My amazing hands help me to _____

My amazing lips allow me to _____

My amazing tummy means I can _____

My amazing feet help me to _____

My amazing face is _____

This is me . . .

My amazing body is just what people see on the outside. On the inside I am . . .

_____

_____

Activity 3.4
I Am Special

Read and complete the sentences below.

I am special because . . . _____
_____
_____

My friends like me because . . . _____
_____
_____

My teacher thinks I am good at . . . _____
_____
_____

I feel good about myself when . . . _____
_____
_____

I am a good friend because . . . _____
_____
_____

I am a good classmate because . . . _____
_____
_____

I am best at . . . _____
_____
_____

Activity 3.5
Things that I Like About Me

Draw a picture of yourself in the middle of the page.

Around the outside of the drawing, label all of the things that you like about yourself. These might be things that you can see, but also could be about your character and all the wonderful things that you have inside.

Activity 3.6
Strengths Cards

Which of these words would you use to describe yourself?

If you had to pick a top three that are most like you, which would you choose and why?

Loyal	Kind	Thoughtful	Generous
Conscientious	Considerate	Helpful	Friendly
Gentle	Brave	Calm	Cooperative
Sporty	Patient	Loving	Adventurous
Fun	Organised	Confident	Sensible
Quirky	Strong	Different	Resourceful
Resilient	Wise	Hard-working	Caring

My three strengths are:

_____   _____   _____

Activity 3.7
Friendship Definitions!

Make two lists!

Things a good friend does . . .	Things a good friend doesn't do . . .

Stop, think & reflect!

How do you rate your skills as a friend?

```
0    1    2    3    4    5    6    7    8    9    10
Not good                    Fair                 Excellent
```

What skills do you need to improve? Who can help you?

_____

_____

Activity 3.8
Building Friendship Skills

Think about the important people and friends in your life. Put their names in the boxes along the top of the grid.

I get on well with:

Name					
Always					
Usually					
Sometimes					
Not often					
Never					

The three best ways for making friends feel valued and appreciated are:

1 _____
2 _____
3 _____

The things I can do to improve my communication skills as a friend are:

1 _____
2 _____
3 _____

Activity 3.8
Building Friendship Skills

Choose one of the things you think you can improve and make a plan.
_____

My plan for improving my communication skills is to:
_____
_____

Name a person that you think can help you improve your skills and say why you think they can help:

_____ will help me by _____
_____

I will improve my communication skills by this date: _____

I will celebrate my achievement with [*insert name of a close friend/someone important to you*]

_____

Activity 3.9
Managing Conflict

There are four main ways of managing conflict:

1. Aggression
2. Mediation
3. Withdrawal
4. Negotiation

Discuss each of these with a partner.

Then decide on and write down the strengths and weaknesses of each approach.

Aggression	
Strengths	Weaknesses

Mediation	
Strengths	Weaknesses

Withdrawal	
Strengths	Weaknesses

Negotiation	
Strengths	Weaknesses

Activity 3.10
Coping with Conflict

The conflict I would like to sort out is _____
_____

Who is involved? _____

Because of the conflict I feel:

1 _____

2 _____

3 _____

Because of the conflict the other person probably feels:

1 _____

2 _____

3 _____

My next steps to sorting this out are:

1 _____

2 _____

3 _____

If that doesn't work I will:

1 _____

2 _____

3 _____

The outcome I would like is _____
_____

I will know when the conflict has been sorted out because _____
_____

4 Effective Thinking Activities

Cognitive Behavioural Therapy

Helping children become aware of the ways in which thoughts can influence emotions and behaviour is one of the most valuable lessons we can give them. Cognitive Behavioural therapy (CBT) can help children to reframe how they identify, interpret and evaluate their emotional and behavioural reactions to negative experiences (Rae, 2016).

Realising that emotions and behaviours can be regulated and managed is empowering and can lead to improvements in self-control, emotion regulation, coping skills, and emotional awareness during this critical developmental stage.

Cognitive Behavioural Therapy (CBT) has been found to be effective for a range of mental health problems, including mood-related disorders (e.g., depression, low self-esteem, low confidence) and anxiety-related problems (e.g., anxiety, panic, eating disorders – such as anorexia nervosa, bulimia nervosa, binge-eating – obsessive compulsive disorder (OCD), post-traumatic stress disorder (PTSD)) and other emotional and behavioural problems (e.g., bereavement, relationship problems, sleep disorders).

The focus

CBT focuses on the role that thoughts play regarding both emotions and behaviour and advocates that changes in thought processes can have a significant effect upon altering behaviours. CBT is based on the idea that the way we think about situations can affect the way we feel and behave. For example, if you interpret a situation negatively then you might experience negative emotions as a result, and those bad feelings might then lead you to behave in a certain way.

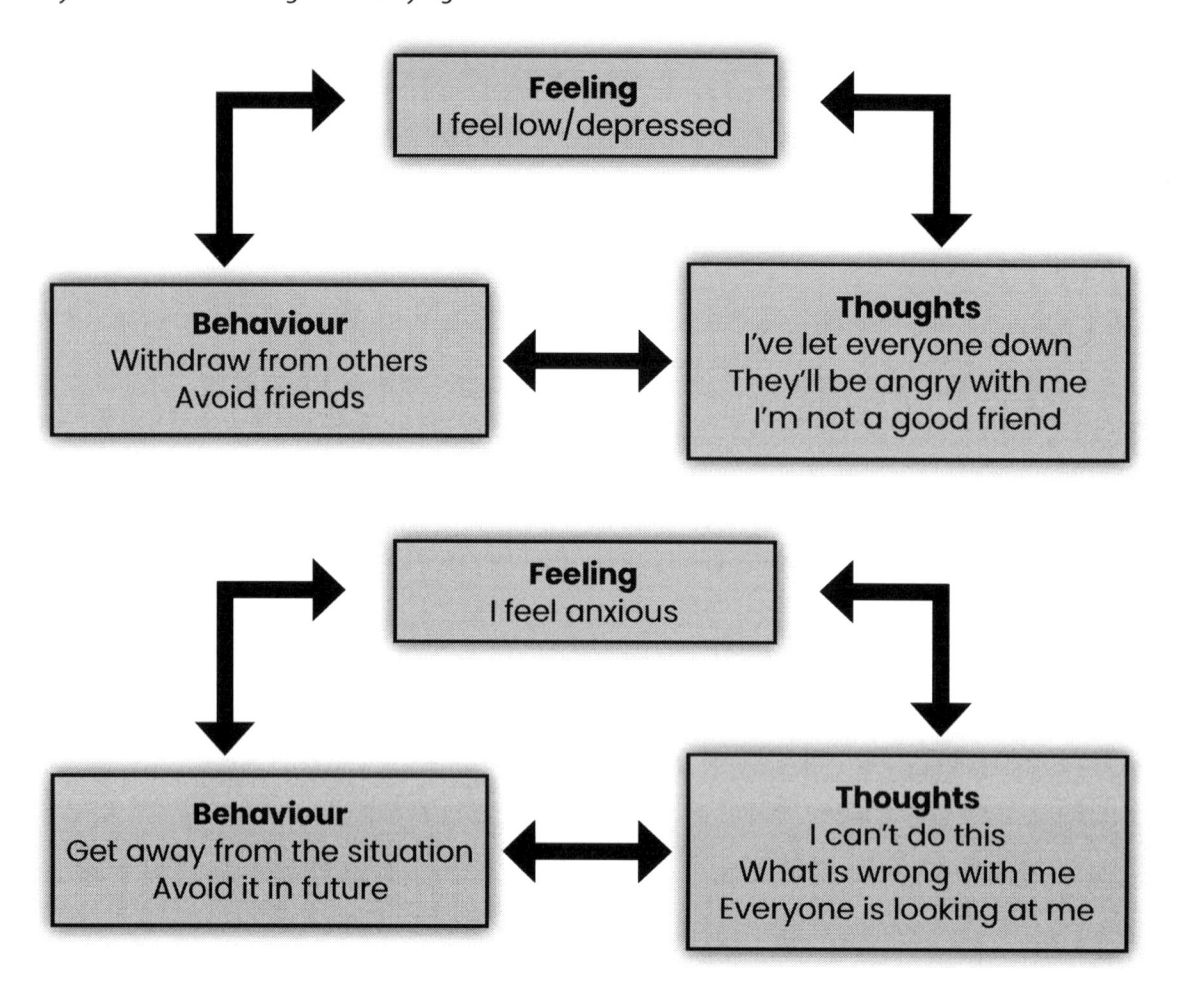

```
        Feeling
    I feel low/depressed

Behaviour                    Thoughts
Withdraw from others         I've let everyone down
Avoid friends                They'll be angry with me
                             I'm not a good friend


        Feeling
      I feel anxious

Behaviour                    Thoughts
Get away from the situation  I can't do this
Avoid it in future           What is wrong with me
                             Everyone is looking at me
```

This approach provides individuals with a way of talking about themselves, their world and the people who inhabit it, so that they are more able to understand how their behaviour affects both their thoughts and feelings.

The tools and strategies employed in this approach are easily accessible to children and young people alike.

The issue

We know that young people are frequently flooded with anxious and negative thoughts and doubts. These messages will often reinforce a state of inadequacy and/or low levels of self-esteem. The process of CBT helps to support young people in reconsidering these negative assumptions. It also allows them to *learn how* to change their self-perceptions in order to improve their mental and emotional state – this is the key aim of this kind of intervention. Changing negative thought patterns or opinions will ultimately help young people to become more able to control and change their behaviours, but this does take practice.

ABC

The CBT approach breaks a problem into three smaller parts:

A is the **activating event**, often referred to as the 'trigger' – the thing that causes you to engage in the negative thinking.

B represents these negative **beliefs**, which can include thoughts, rules and demands, and the meanings the individual attaches to both external and internal events.

C is for the **consequences**, or emotions, and the behaviours and physical sensations accompanying these different emotions. It is important to highlight and discuss with children how the way that they think about a problem can affect how they feel physically and emotionally. It can also alter what they do about it. Therefore, the key aim for CBT is to break the negative, vicious cycle that some students may find themselves in. For example, if you think that you will get your work wrong you feel angry, and then you do not give it a try in case it is wrong.

Cognitive Restructuring

The purpose of this technique is to change cognitive distortions (irrational negative thoughts and beliefs someone has about different situations) and to increase positive self-talk. Normally, there will be some type of event that will trigger the irrational thought. While the event cannot be changed, the way the child looks at the event can be. An example could be a child working hard on a project or test and not receiving as high a grade as they expected. A child will see their efforts as useless and may start to think, 'I'm useless', or 'There is no point in trying.' Other irrational negative thoughts could include:

- I can't do anything well
- Things never work out for me
- Nobody likes me
- I'm dumb
- Something's wrong with me
- I can't make any friends
- I'm worthless

These thoughts need to be recognised and countered. Often the child will not even realise exactly what they are saying and how irrational these thoughts are. It is one of the main focuses of this technique to recognise the thoughts that will cause the anxiety. However, it is also important to not counter them with equally irrational positive thoughts. For example, it would not be proper to counter, 'Nobody likes me', with, 'No, everyone *does* like you.' It is important to be **realistic** with the replacement thought. 'Well not *everyone* likes you, but you know some people do; your mother and sister love you', would be a better approach.

It is important that these negative attitudes do not form part of the child's habitual thought patterns. The child will begin to believe them fully and this leads to depression, feelings of worthlessness, and a loss of direction. It could also precipitate avoidance or even panic attacks in the child. You can correct the child whenever you hear it as a part of their speech, and work to have them recognise it themselves. Encourage them to recognise the good things they do instead. Make sure they know there is no shame in congratulating themselves for a job well done.

Activity 4.1
Know Yourself!

Thoughts & feelings

THOUGHTS that make me feel positive!	THOUGHTS that make me feel negative!
🍃 _____	🍃 _____
🍃 _____	🍃 _____
🍃 _____	🍃 _____

ACTIVITIES that make me feel positive!	ACTIVITIES that make me feel negative!
🍃 _____	🍃 _____
🍃 _____	🍃 _____
🍃 _____	🍃 _____

Activity 4.2
Comfortable Feelings Daily Diary

Sometimes we think of feelings as simply being good or bad. Perhaps it is more helpful to think of them as being comfortable or uncomfortable?

When do you feel **comfortable**? Make a list of times and places and people that have made you feel comfortable.

Use the daily diary format below.

	Time	People	Place
Monday			
Tuesday			
Wednesday			

Page 1 of 2

Activity 4.2
Comfortable Feelings Daily Diary

	Time	People	Place
Thursday			
Friday			
Saturday			
Sunday			

Do you notice anything?

How can you make sure you have more of these comfortable feelings every day?

What can you do? Who can help you?

Activity 4.3
My ABC

Write or draw your own ABCs, using the three boxes.

Adversity	Belief	Consequences
Something happens …	What I tell myself …	How do I feel?

Adversity	Belief	Consequences
Something happens …	What I tell myself …	How do I feel?

Adversity	Belief	Consequences
Something happens …	What I tell myself …	How do I feel?

Activity 4.4
Positive Acts

When you feel low, or fed up, or sad, there are six things you can do to stop it taking over.

1. **Catch the thought**
   Thought catching: what can you say to yourself to stop that bad mood from getting worse?

2. **Act fast**
   What one thing can you do now to begin to sort out the situation so that it doesn't get worse?

3. **Distract yourself**
   Do something else. What can you do now to get your mind off the situation that has prompted your bad mood?

4. **Do something different**
   Take your mind off it. Talk about something else with a friend. How can you make that happen? What can you discuss that will help change your mood?

5. **Complete an act of kindness**
   Do something for someone else. When people do things for other people, they have more meaning in their lives and feel better than when they do things for themselves. What could you do?

6. **Exercise**
   Get moving. Take some exercise so that you can't think about that bad mood. What will you do?

Work with a partner to identify four more strategies you can use.

Activity 4.5
Controlling Thoughts

FACTS

- We listen to our thoughts a lot.

- We often accept negative thoughts as 'the truth', without really challenging them.

- These thoughts can become louder and it becomes harder to hear the positive thoughts.

- The more we listen to them, the more uncomfortable and down we feel, and the less we do – it's a TRAP!!

THE SOLUTION: DISTRACTION

- Distraction helps you take your mind off the negative thoughts.

- Distraction helps you take CONTROL of your thoughts by thinking of something else.

- You DROWN OUT those negative thoughts by ensuring your mind does what YOU want it to!

What can you do to distract yourself? Make a list!

_____
_____
_____
_____
_____

Activity 4.6
Thought Detective 1

Be a thought detective. Find the EVIDENCE for your thoughts! Record FOUR negative thoughts and the evidence you have for and against them!

DAY and TIME	THOUGHT Rate how much you believe it using the 1–10 THOUGHT SCALE (1=not at all 10=totally)	EVIDENCE FOR the thought	EVIDENCE AGAINST the thought
(1)			
(2)			
(3)			
(4)			

Activity 4.7
Thought Detective 2: Friends Can Help!

Use friends to help you be a thought detective!

Find the EVIDENCE for your thoughts! Record FOUR negative thoughts and the evidence you have for and against them – remember to put yourself in your friend's shoes!

THOUGHT	What would my best friend say to me about this thought?	What I would say to my best friend if they had this thought?	How much do I believe this thought now? Use the 1–10 THOUGHT SCALE (1=not at all 10=totally)
(1)			
(2)			
(3)			
(4)			

Activity 4.8
'What Ifs' Game

Many of our worries about the future begin with the phrase, 'What If . . .?'

But often we never actually answer that question!

Take the time to think through each of these scenarios to realise that there is always an answer to that question – and it's usually much less scary than you think!

What if . . . I have nobody to play with in the playground?
_____

What if . . . the work is too hard and I can't do it?
_____

What if . . . I feel sick in class?
_____

What if . . . I get bullied?
_____

What if . . . I hurt myself?
_____

What if . . . everybody laughs at me?
_____

What if . . . I have a panic attack at school?
_____

Now make up some of your own, based on your worries, and see if you can answer them too.

What if . . .? _____

What if . . .? _____

What if . . .? _____

Activity 4.9

Good Decisions for a Positive Future

Stop, think & reflect!

There are people who I can talk to when I have to make an important decision. They are:

_____

_____

_____

Read the following statements and tick the ones that you use to make decisions.

I think through all the pros and cons		I think it through	
I go along with other people		I panic	
I can't make up my mind		I toss a coin	
I do nothing and try and forget about it		I trust my instinct	
I get confused and can't think straight		I don't care; whatever	
I get all the information and then I decide		I always know what is best	
I talk to other people			

Give each of these decision-making styles a score out of 10.
10 = excellent; 5 = OK; 1 = not good

	Score
Toss a coin	
Just do what others want	
Do nothing and wait and see what happens	
Don't think about it, just do what feels right	
Do whatever will make everybody else happy	
Do the first thing that comes into your head	
Think for a very long time before you make a decision and make a list of pros and cons	

Activity 4.10
Making a Priority Goal for My Positive Future!

My priority goal is _____

These are the steps to achieving my goal:

1 _____
2 _____
3 _____
4 _____
5 _____

These are the people who will help me:

1 _____
2 _____
3 _____

These will be my rewards along the way:

1 _____
2 _____
3 _____

If something doesn't work out I will:

1 _____
2 _____
3 _____

When I reach my goal, I will celebrate by _____

P This page may be photocopied for instructional use only.
A Recovery Toolbox for Wellbeing for Primary-Aged Children © Tina Rae & Ali D'Amario 2021

5 Anxiety-Busting Activities

What is Anxiety?

Anxiety is a normal response to a perceived threat and includes physical, emotional and mental responses, such as an increase in adrenalin, feelings of worry and confusion, and thoughts about danger and catastrophic outcomes. Normal levels of anxiety can assist people to be more focused and motivated, and to solve problems more efficiently. However, **chronic or high levels of anxiety** can reduce a person's capacity to respond appropriately or effectively to stressful situations or even normal routine activities. For example, a highly anxious person may experience constant physical feelings of panic and may seek to avoid anything that might trigger their anxiety (such as being alone, going to school, or talking in front of a group).

Anxiety may be triggered in many different ways. Sources of anxiety may include (but are not limited to) fear of:

- Social situations
- Negative evaluation and rejection
- Performing in public
- A specific object or situation (e.g., storms or lightning/thunder, insects, blood)
- Separation from a parent/carer
- A parent/carer being harmed
- Harm to oneself
- Academic performance and exams
- Starting school or work
- The future (what will happen, how it might turn out)

Anxiety may manifest as a number of physical symptoms, including muscle tension, shaking/trembling and heart palpitations, sweating/flushing, or feeling very hot or cold, amongst many others. In addition, children and young people experiencing anxiety may display a number of behavioural symptoms, including withdrawing from friends and family, avoidance of particular situations and negative thoughts or pessimism. Due to the way in which the brain develops, young children are particularly prone to responding with heightened emotions and find it more difficult to understand or regulate these emotions.

Signs of anxiety in young children may include:

- Increased tantrums/meltdowns
- Regression (e.g., in toileting)
- Changes in eating
- Difficulty sleeping
- Being clingy
- More tearful
- Complaining of tummy aches, or feeling unwell

Top Tips for Supporting Children who Are Feeling Anxious

1. Often children lack the emotional vocabulary to be able to communicate their feelings to you, and therefore they show their anxiety through their behaviour (e.g. tantrums or meltdowns, controlling behaviour, defiance). Labelling their emotions for them and empathising can really help them to start to identify the feelings for themselves so that they can communicate in a more adaptive way as they develop. See Appendix 4 on Emotion Coaching for more information.

2. Teach children about what is happening in their bodies when they feel anxious, and why (fight or flight). Knowing that the feeling is normal, and that they can control their breathing to reduce the physiological symptoms, can help the anxiety to feel less frightening.

3. Ensure that you have a good bedtime routine in place which helps them to calm down. For example, a bath around an hour before bed to ensure optimal core body temperature for a restful night's sleep, no screens before bed, and read them a bedtime story to help them to settle. Sleep allows us to better regulate our emotions, so a well-rested child is more likely to be a calm one!

4. Help them to face things that make them anxious by gently teaching them to problem solve around their fears. For example, if they are afraid of dogs, modelling calm behaviour around a known, calm dog to show them that they are not dangerous. This is much more empowering than protecting them and assisting them in avoiding the things that they are afraid of, as this sends the message that the feared situation is dangerous for them and that they cannot cope with it, meaning that the anxiety is more likely to persist.

5 Keep your calm! It can be exceptionally difficult to keep calm yourself when faced with an anxious child who seems as though they are being defiant or difficult. Just try to remember that they are still learning how to control those big emotions. It's our job to show them how.

Whilst anxiety is a normal reaction to stressful events or change, if you are concerned that anxiety is affecting your child's behaviour and thoughts every day and interfering with their ability to function socially, or at home or school, you should consult with a medical professional as this may be indicative of an anxiety disorder (see Appendix 3, 'Stress, Anxiety Disorder & Depression Information').

Activity 5.1
Body Outline

Identifying the places on your body where you experience physical sensations of anxiety (e.g., butterflies in your tummy) can help you to quickly recognise when you are feeling anxious in the future.

Draw on the body the feelings that you get when you feel worried about something.

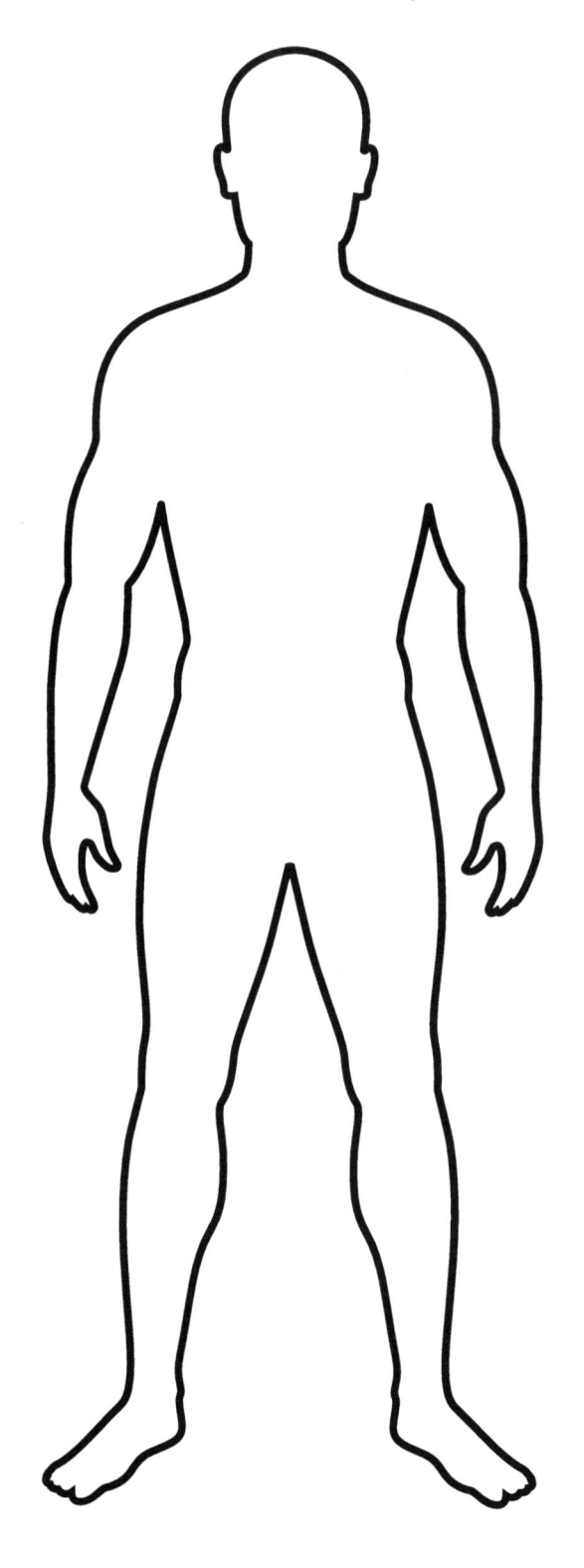

Activity 5.2
My Worries

Write down the worries that are troubling you in the bubbles below. Order them from the biggest worry, down to the smallest worry.

Activity 5.3
Things that I Can Control

Often we spend lots of time worrying about things that are beyond our control and that we can do nothing about.

It is natural to want to have control when we feel uncertain or anxious, and there are some things that we DO have control over. Perhaps we can focus on those, rather than the things that are NOT in our control?

In our control

My actions

Showing kindness to others

Looking after myself

Asking for help

Out of our control

The actions of others

The views of others

The feelings of others

The words that other people use

What can you do today to help you to feel calm and in control?

Activity 5.4
Hidden Feelings

Look at the character . . .

How do you think they are feeling?
_____
_____
_____
_____

What tells you that they are feeling that way?
_____
_____
_____
_____

Why might they be feeling that way?
_____
_____
_____
_____

What might help them to feel better?
_____
_____

Activity 5.5
Anxiety Checklist!

Just check out how you feel. If you are feelings lots of the things on this list, then ask an adult for help and talk it through. Do not let it get bigger and bigger!

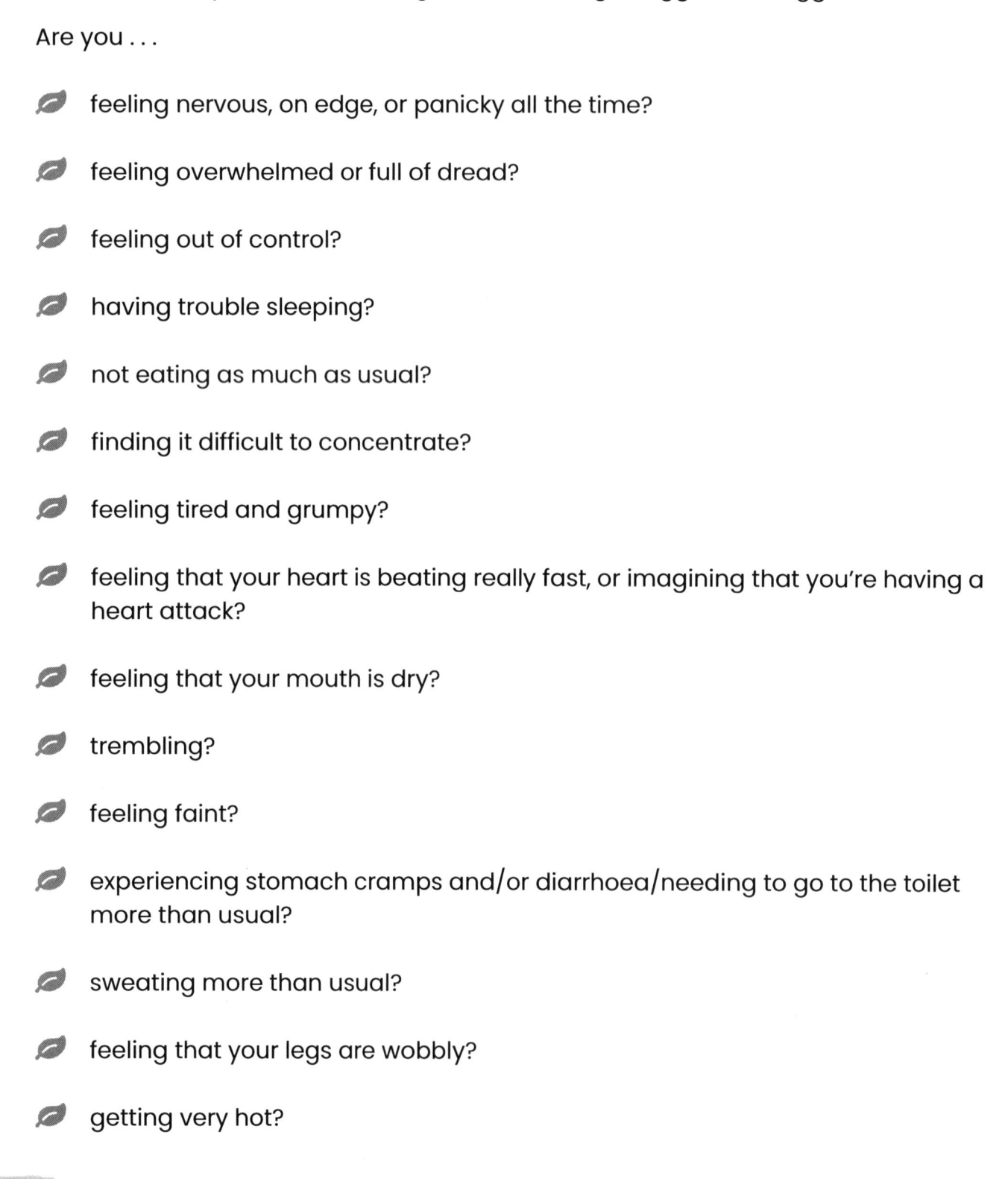

Are you . . .

- feeling nervous, on edge, or panicky all the time?
- feeling overwhelmed or full of dread?
- feeling out of control?
- having trouble sleeping?
- not eating as much as usual?
- finding it difficult to concentrate?
- feeling tired and grumpy?
- feeling that your heart is beating really fast, or imagining that you're having a heart attack?
- feeling that your mouth is dry?
- trembling?
- feeling faint?
- experiencing stomach cramps and/or diarrhoea/needing to go to the toilet more than usual?
- sweating more than usual?
- feeling that your legs are wobbly?
- getting very hot?

Activity 5.6
Calming Cards

Think of all the techniques you can use to calm yourself down. You might use colouring, counting, best breathing, running, hand breathing (Activity 1.2), grounding the senses (Activity 1.4), and so on.

Now use the template below and cut the sections up into separate cards. You could illustrate them on one side and write down a technique on the other side.

Keep the cards in a little box and choose one technique whenever you begin to feel anxious.

Activity 5.7
Scaling

How anxious would you feel, on a scale of 1 to 10 (with 1 being 'not at all anxious' and 10 being 'extremely anxious') in the following situations . . .

- Before school   _____
- At break time   _____
- During lessons   _____
- At lunchtime   _____
- At home-time   _____
- When I get home   _____

Pick one situation in which you would like to feel less anxious.

_____

_____

Which number on the scale would you like to get to? _____

What could you do that might help you to get there?

_____

_____

_____

What could someone else do to help you?

_____

_____

_____

Activity 5.8
Worry Eaters!

Draw a worry monster who can eat up the worries!

Then make up a story about the monster and what they do to get rid of the worry.

Think about the strategies you use to keep calm and try to include some of them in your story frame below.

Activity 5.9
Exercise Reduces Anxiety!

If we exercise every day we will feel fitter and healthier. We will also feel happier as exercise boosts our happy chemicals in our brains and in our bodies!

SO KEEP ON MOVING!

Find out what exercise suits you and motivates you: dance, gym, football, and so on.

Then work out a weekly timetable and complete the exercise diary below:

	My exercise of choice	Time	Feelings in the exercise	Feelings after
Monday				
Tuesday				
Wednesday				
Thursday				
Friday				
Saturday				
Sunday				

Thought-storm!

Work with friends to identify as many different physical activities that could help you keep fit as you can (e.g., skipping, judo, trampolining, taekwondo, swimming, kick-boxing, surfing, jazz, ballet, etc.).

Activity 5.10

My Anxiety Playlist

Make a list of all the lovely calming music that helps to de-stress you when you are beginning to feel anxious.

Then make up your playlist and use it!

1. _____
2. _____
3. _____
4. _____
5. _____
6. _____
7. _____
8. _____
9. _____
10. _____
11. _____
12. _____
13. _____
14. _____
15. _____
16. _____
17. _____
18. _____
19. _____
20. _____

6 Transition Activities

Whether you are supporting a child who is transitioning back to junior school, a new school year and teacher, or moving to secondary school, think of transition as a process rather than a one-off event. They will need careful preparation beforehand and it may take a while before they feel settled. Change is a stressor for all of us and, when we already feel anxious, change can feel particularly overwhelming. According to neuroscientist, Dr Bruce Perry (2020), we are most able to tolerate change when it feels predictable and within our control. For this reason, we have included some activities that will help you and your child to plan for changes, and maintain a consistent, predictable routine within your day.

We must not forget that this transition is likely to be harder than most, following all of the messages that children have received around 'staying safe at home', and the implicit suggestion that other children and adults pose a threat to us. Therefore, it is essential that children are supported in feeling that school and the outside world are safe places to be, so that they have the confidence to explore, play and learn.

Within the current pandemic, it is likely that some children will find it difficult to separate from their parents after so long together. It is important to accept, validate and empathise with the child, rather than trying to distract them away from their very understandable emotion.

The following general guidance may also be helpful in easing the transition:

- The child may benefit through having access to pictures of the school, their teachers, and opportunities to meet with other children in their class (even if done virtually). You could also prepare them by allowing them to try on their uniform and get used to their school shoes, as well as doing some test-runs of the journey to school.

- Communication between home and school is key to ensure a smooth transition. Parents know their children the best and any transition document or meeting should allow for discussion of how the child shows their anxiety and what helps them to feel calm. At this time, it will also be essential to discuss their individual experience of lockdown and how this may impact upon the transition.

- Make time to speak to your child about their worries about the transition, but also the opportunities for this new beginning. Try to change the narrative from being one of change and worry, to one of resilience and hope, using the activities below.

Activity 6.1
Coming Back to School

Name _____

This emoji is the one that says how I feel about coming back to school!

Three things I have enjoyed about being at home:

1 _____

2 _____

3 _____

Three things I have missed about school:

1 _____

2 _____

3 _____

Three things that I would like you to know about me:

1 _____

2 _____

3 _____

Three things that I am most looking forward to:

1 _____

2 _____

3 _____

Activity 6.2
Change is Good!

Sometimes changes can feel a bit scary, but change can also be exciting and give us new opportunities.

Think of a time that you had a big change in your life, write about it below.

_____
_____

How did you feel before?

_____
_____

What did you do to help you to cope with the change?

_____
_____

How did you feel afterwards?

_____
_____

What advice would you give someone else who was about to deal with a big change?

_____
_____

Do you have any more changes that are likely to happen soon?

_____
_____

How could you help yourself to be ready to take on this change?

_____
_____

Activity 6.3
Problem Postcards

Cut out the postcards.

Record your concern about going back to school or making a transition on one side, then swap with a partner and try to write down a solution for each other on the reverse of the cards!

DISCUSS AND ASK EACH OTHER FOR HELP AND IDEAS.

✂ cut along dotted lines

Problem 1	Problem 2
PTO for solution	PTO for solution
Problem 3	Problem 4
PTO for solution	PTO for solution

Page 1 of 2

Activity 6.3
Problem Postcards

Problem 5	Problem 6
PTO for solution	PTO for solution
Problem 7	Problem 8
PTO for solution	PTO for solution

Page 2 of 2

Activity 6.4
Scale It!

How worried am I about the transition to my school or a new school?

```
0    1    2    3    4    5    6    7    8    9    10
|----|----|----|----|----|----|----|----|----|----|
☺                        😐                        ☹
Very                    Quite                  Not worried
worried                 worried                   at all
```

I am at _____ on the scale.

I am at this point because:
_____
_____

I would like to be at _____ on the scale.

In order to get there, I need to do the following:

1 _____

2 _____

3 _____

4 _____

These are the people who can help me to do this:
_____
_____

I will know when I have moved up the scale because:
_____
_____

Activity 6.5
Changes: I Can Cope with Them!

Look at each of the changes that you will cope with during transition. DISCUSS in a small group and try to record ways you will cope with each change on the chart below.

Changes	Coping Strategies What can I do and who can help me?
Uniform	
Travelling to school	
Equipment	
My class group	
Finding my way around	
Homework	
School rules and safety rules	
Work issues	

Activity 6.6
Connecting with Others

Think about the people in your life and then answer the following questions:

If I need help with my homework, I would ask _____

If I have a quarrel with my best friend, I would talk to _____

If I felt lonely I would _____

If I got lost I would _____

If I needed money I would _____

If I didn't understand the homework I would _____

Complete the following three sentences with your own examples:

If I _____ I would _____

If I _____ I would _____

If I _____ I would _____

These people will help me to cope:

1 _____

2 _____

3 _____

4 _____

5 _____

Activity 6.7
A Positive Note to Me

Write a positive note to yourself! Record all the things that make you feel glad to be you and glad to be going to your school!

Put it in an envelope and keep it safe. Read it when you feel that you have had a difficult day and things have made you feel sad.

Dear ...

Activity 6.8
Personal Information for My Teachers

My name is _____

🍃 I am _____

🍃 I manage better in class when _____
_____

🍃 I find it really hard to _____
_____

🍃 I prefer it when I can work _____
_____

🍃 Please do not ask me to _____
_____

🍃 You can help me by _____
_____

Thank you!

Activity 6.9
Safe Haven

What makes us feel safe at school and at home?

Discuss your ideas in a group and ask your teacher to record your safety rules. Make up a chart to illustarte these.

Think about what makes you:

- Physically safe
- Emotionally safe
- Safe in learning
- Safe in the classroom
- Safe in the playground
- Safe at lunch times
- Safe travelling to and from school

Then think about what you can do to:

- Help yourself stay safe
- Help others to stay safe

Activity 6.10
My Best Future

Who do I want to be in the future?

What do I want to be feeling, thinking and doing?

What do I want to achieve?

Draw yourself as a student in your current class and record your ideas around the edge of the picture frame.

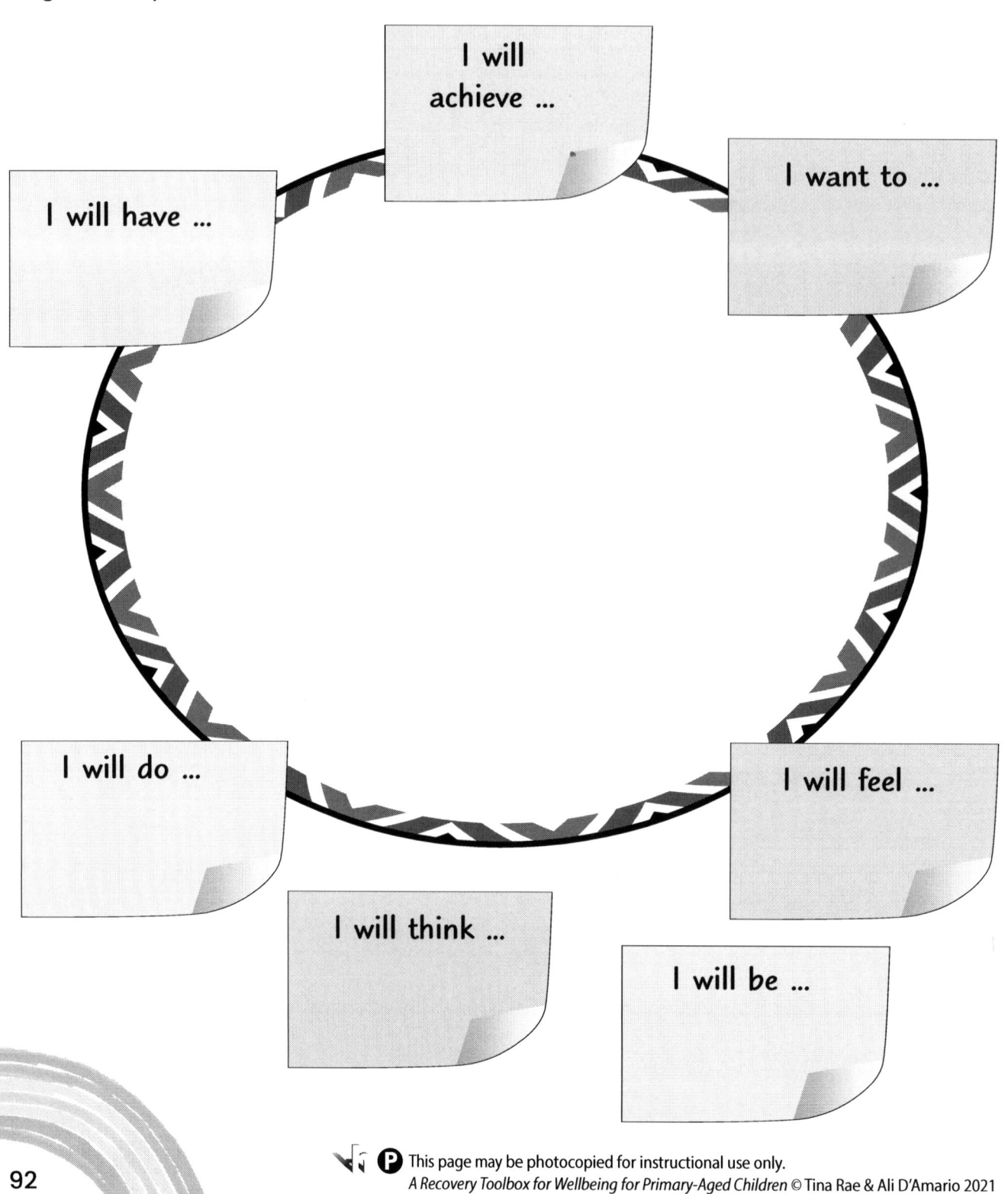

- I will achieve …
- I want to …
- I will have …
- I will do …
- I will think …
- I will feel …
- I will be …

Appendices

1 Helpful Websites … 94

2 Mindfulness Information … … … … … … … … … … … … … … … … … … … 96

3 Stress, Anxiety Disorder & Depression Information … … … … … … … … … … 99

4 Emotion Coaching Information … … … … … … … … … … … … … … … … … 104

5 Using Circle of Friends approaches… … … … … … … … … … … … … … … … 106

6 Trauma Recovery Self-Care Tips … … … … … … … … … … … … … … … … … 110

7 Whole-School Recovery … … … … … … … … … … … … … … … … … … … 113

8 A Recovery Plan to Support School Staff and Carers as Children Return to School … … … 116

Appendix 1
Helpful Websites

Action for Children
actionforchildren.org.uk
Charity supporting children, young people and their families across England

Anxiety UK
anxietyuk.org.uk
03444 775 774 (helpline); 07537 416 905 (text)
Advice and support for people living with anxiety

Beat
beateatingdisorders.co.uk
0808 801 0711 (youthline); 0808 801 0811 (studentline)
Under 18s helpline, webchat and online support groups for people with eating disorders, such as anorexia and bulimia

Childline
childline.org.uk
0800 1111
Support for children and young people in the UK, including a free 24-hour helpline

Hope Again
hopeagain.org.uk
0808 808 1677
Support for young people when someone dies

Kooth
kooth.com
Counsellors available until 10pm every day. Free, safe and anonymous online counselling for young people

Me and My Mind
meandmymind.nhs.uk
Advice and support for young people struggling with unusual experiences, such as hearing voices

Mencap

mencap.org.uk

0808 808 1111

Information and advice for people with a learning disability, families and carers

National Society for the Prevention of Cruelty to Children (NSPCC)

nspcc.org.uk

0800 800 5000; 0800 1111 (18 or under)

Support for children and anyone worried about a child.

OCD Youth

ocdyouth.org

Youth support for young people with obsessive-compulsive disorder (OCD)

On My Mind

annafreud.org/on-my-mind

Information for young people to make informed choices about their mental health and wellbeing

Samaritans

samaritans.org

116 123; jo@samaritans.org

Freepost RSRB-KKBY-CYJK, PO Box 90 90, Stirling FK8 2SA

24-hour emotional support for anyone who needs to talk

The Mix

themix.org.uk

0808 808 4994; 85258 (crisis messenger service, Text THEMIX)

Support and advice for under 25s, including webchat

YoungMinds

youngminds.org.uk

0808 802 5544 (parents helpline); 85258 (crisis messenger service, text YM)

Committed to improving the mental health of babies, children and young people, including support for parents and carers

Appendix 2
Mindfulness Information

What is Mindfulness?

Mindfulness can be characterised as our innate ability to be fully present in the moment – to focus on where we are and what we are doing without allowing other, intrusive thoughts, worries, or fears to permeate our minds. When we are practising Mindfulness, we are impartial and non-judgmental of what is happening around us, and when our minds wander, we redirect our thoughts back to the present moment.

Rae et al., 2017

The benefits of Mindfulness

Sensory Awareness   Practising Mindfulness nurtures the capacity to bring our sensory experience into our consciousness. This enables us to create the space to simply stop and 'be', experiencing the moment in all its fullness. Being able to be in the moment and appreciate the positive sensory experiences that we have is not simply enjoyable, it also elicits positive emotions that feed into overall wellbeing. Recurrently experiencing positive emotions simultaneously broadens our sensory awareness, helping build psychological and emotional resilience overall.

Cognitive Control   The goal of Mindfulness is not to simply eliminate the mind of all thoughts and feelings, but to anchor oneself to what you are currently experiencing in the sensory world. The idea is to allow thoughts to enter the mind quite freely and to simply note these in a non-judgemental and unanalytical manner. This is particularly useful in terms of managing busy minds that are continually barraged with thoughts – Mindfulness enables us to create distance between the thoughts that we have and our cognitive reactions to them. We can have a thought without having to act upon it. We can treat it just simply as a thought.

Emotional Regulation   It is extremely easy to become overwhelmed by intrusive emotional thoughts. These very often reflect uncomfortable situations which caused us to feel angry, embarrassed or stressed. Mindfulness encourages a more de-centred perspective on such feelings. Emotions can be acknowledged and allowed to pass. If we just recognise the feelings, then we provide ourselves with the opportunity to choose how to respond to them rather than reacting automatically, engaging in unconscious patterns of automatic negative thinking.

Acceptance   Treating our thoughts in this non-judgemental and more detached manner is also hugely positive in terms of accepting our thoughts and feelings. This is particularly important as it encourages us to be more tolerant and kinder to ourselves. We do not need to beat ourselves up for having negative or intrusive thoughts or feelings; we simply must accept them and know that we need to learn to be kinder to ourselves in both the short and longer terms.

Attention Regulation   Given the fact that Mindfulness does not demand that we clear our minds of all thoughts and feelings, but rather allow them to pass by and be noted, this in effect provides us with training in how to regulate and direct at will our attention.

Why teaching Mindfulness to children is important

Sadly, for many of today's children, there is little opportunity to experience the wonderful world of boredom. They do not have the space to switch off, tune the world out, and find their inner creativity. The rise in mental health challenges like anxiety and depression are now thought to be linked to this hyper-vigilance and more complex social context. It is also clearly currently linked to the ongoing anxiety children and young people are experiencing as they navigate this global pandemic.

It is therefore a real positive that more and more teachers are starting to incorporate Mindfulness into their classroom curriculums, and the benefits have been staggering. Teaching Mindfulness to children can:

- decrease feelings of stress and anxiety
- improve focus and concentration
- help with impulsivity
- improve self-regulation
- develop empathy
- reduce aggression
- improve sleep

Investigating why, how and when to use Mindfulness is therefore immensely helpful for both professionals and parents/carers who are seeking to support children and young people currently.

Six tips for teaching Mindfulness to children

1. **Practise Mindfulness yourself.** Before we can successfully teach anything to our children, we need to have a working understanding of the concept ourselves. Take the time to learn about Mindfulness and how to practise it, since children learn by example, and the more you demonstrate the positive effects Mindfulness has on you and your wellbeing, the more interested and open the children will be to trying it for themselves.

2. **Get the children involved.** As with most activities, the more involved children are, the better. Set aside some time to explain what Mindfulness is and why it is important, and then make a 'Mindfulness Calendar' that outlines which days you are going to try different exercises and activities, and take the time to evaluate them all to decide which ones you all enjoy and would like to try again.

3. **Start small.** Remember that Mindfulness does not need to be a long and elaborate affair, and you are most likely to maintain their interest in practising together if you start small.

4. **Make it a habit.** Allocate time each day to practise Mindfulness together, and make sure to choose a time that works best for you all – first thing in the morning, after lunch, and so on – and then make it a habit. The more consistent you are the more benefits you will see.

5. **Get moving.** Contrary to popular belief, Mindfulness activities are not all about sitting quietly with your eyes closed while meditating. There are lots of Mindfulness exercises for children that involve movement, and if your children initially struggle to sit still, these may be a better option for them.

6. **Be patient.** And do not expect a miracle. Teaching Mindfulness to children can be extremely beneficial, but remember that change takes time and it is unlikely that you will see an overnight transformation. As with most things, consistency is key.

Appendix 3
Stress, Anxiety Disorder & Depression Information

Stress

Defining stress is quite a difficult and complex process given that it means different things to different people (in a similar vein as happiness, failure or success). Even though stress is a normal part of everyday life, too much stress makes young people become anxious, exhausted, tired and unable to function appropriately, both inside and outside school.

All of us have an optimum stress level, which allows us to function effectively and efficiently in our daily lives – what is vital is that we learn how to recognise our own stress levels and develop coping strategies when we are experiencing higher levels of stress. This will enable us to maintain a healthy balance of tension, growth, rest and self-nurturing. We need to be able to focus and build up reactions that reduce stress alongside understanding, acknowledging and coping effectively with the sources of our individual stresses.

Children who are experiencing higher levels of stress may exhibit the following behaviours:

- More aggressive or withdrawn behaviour
- Feeling tearful
- Eating disorders
- Self-harming behaviours
- School-attendance problems
- Need for attention
- Dropping performance
- Lying
- Heightened aggression

As well as the obvious stressors that occur in school, children may face stressors outside school, such as poverty, family disharmony, bereavement, abuse and a change of home or school.

Anxiety disorders

When the anxiety experienced by a child starts to affect their general functioning, they may not just be feeling stressed – they may be suffering from an **anxiety disorder**. Anxiety disorders are considered serious mental health problems and are one of the most common types of mental health concerns for children and young people. Anxiety disorders are so common that one-in-four people will experience one or more anxiety disorders during their lifetime. The anxiety disorders include:

- **Generalised Anxiety Disorder (GAD)** Excessive and persistent anxiety about events and activities related to work, study, health, finances, family issues or other general concerns. People who have GAD have difficulty controlling worry, and the associated physical and emotional symptoms such as restlessness, fatigue, difficulties in concentrating, muscle tension and sleep disturbance. GAD affects approximately 5 per cent of people at some point in their lives

- **Panic Attacks & Panic Disorder** Panic attacks include multiple physical and cognitive anxiety symptoms in the absence of an external threat. A panic attack can include shortness of breath, accelerated heart rate, trembling, sweating, dizziness, and fear of going crazy or dying. Fear of panic attacks in public places may lead to *agoraphobia*.

- **Obsessive Compulsive Disorder (OCD)** OCD is recurrent and persistent thoughts, impulses or images that are intrusive and unwanted (obsessions), and repetitive and ritualistic behaviours or mental acts that are time consuming and distressing (compulsions), for example: fears of contamination or harm to self or others; excessive hand washing, showering, checking, or repeating routine actions. OCD affects about 3 per cent of people at some point in their lives.

- **Post-Traumatic Stress Disorder (PTSD)** PTSD may develop after exposure to a distressing and traumatic event or ongoing traumatic situation. Recurrent thoughts, images and nightmares of the trauma occur, as well as changes in mood. Other symptoms include emotional reactivity, memory and concentration difficulties. Around 8 per cent of people are affected by PTSD at some point in their lives

- **Social Phobia** Anticipatory worry and avoidance of social and performance situations, due to fears of scrutiny and judgment by others, and fear of behaving in a way that is embarrassing or humiliating. Physical anxiety symptoms commonly occur.

- **Specific Phobia(s)** Excessively fear of a particular thing or type of situation. Phobias can start at any age and a person may have more than one phobia. Common phobias include:
  - *Claustrophobia*, or fear of small spaces such as fitting rooms
  - *Zoophobia*, or fear of animals
  - *Acrophobia*, or fear of heights such as flying
  - *Agrophobia*, or fear open spaces or being in situations where escape might be difficult

8 ways a child's anxiety shows up as something else

1. **Anger** – the perception of danger, stress or opposition is enough to trigger the fight or flight responses leaving your child angry and without a way to communicate why.

2. **Difficulty Sleeping** – in children, having difficulty falling asleep or staying asleep is one of the hallmark characteristics of anxiety.

3. **Defiance** – unable to communicate what is really going on, it is easy to interpret the child's defiance as a lack of discipline instead of an attempt to control a situation where they feel anxious or helpless.

4. **Chandeliering** – Chandeliering is when a seemingly calm person suddenly flies off the handle for no reason. They have pushes hurt and anxiety so deep for so long that a seemingly innocent comment or event suddenly sends them straight through the chandelier.

5. **Lack of Focus** – children with anxiety are often so caught up in their own thoughts that they do not pay attention to what is going on around them.

6. **Avoidance** – children who are trying to avoid a particular person, place or task often end up experiencing more of whatever it is they are avoiding.

7. **Negativity** – people with anxiety tend to experience negative thoughts at a much greater intensity than positive ones.

8. **Over planning** – over planning and defiance go hand in hand in their root cause, where anxiety can cause some children to try to take back control through defiant behaviour, it can cause others to over plan for situations where planning is minimal or unnecessary.

9 things to say to your anxious child to reassure them and help them to calm down

1 I'm here with you. You're safe.
2 Do you want to do some dancing or running to get rid of the worried energy?
3 Tell me about it.
4 What would you like to say to your worry? What might your worry say back? Then what?
5 Let's draw it.
6 What does it feel like in your body? Where is the worry? How big is it?
7 Match your breaths to mine.
8 Let's think up some endings for what could happen. (anxious ones, goofy ones AND realistic ones)
9 What's something we could do to help you feel better?

Depression

Depression is when a child's mood is very low, with no obvious cause. Between the ages of 8 and puberty, around 2 to 4 per cent of children are diagnosed with depression; after puberty it is around 4 to 8 per cent, and it is more common in girls than boys.

The symptoms of depression are very similar to those in adults:

- Depressed mood most of the day, every day
- Loss of interest or pleasure in activities
- Significant weight loss, when not dieting, or weight gain
- A decrease or increase in appetite
- Frequent insomnia or sleeping too much
- Extreme restlessness or lethargy
- Fatigue or loss of energy
- Feelings of worthlessness or inappropriate guilt
- Diminished ability to think or concentrate
- Recurrent thoughts of death and suicidal thoughts

Children are likely to seem more irritable than sad, and they are more likely to have insomnia than sleep too much. You may notice that the child does not want to do the things they usually enjoy, avoids people, complains they cannot sleep well, and exhibits a change in their eating patterns. They might start being critical about themselves, or say they feel useless. They will not do as well as usual at school, because they cannot concentrate and do not have the energy to finish work.

Appendix 3 – Stress, Anxiety Disorder & Depression Information

Some of the symptoms of depression – particularly restlessness and finding it difficult to concentrate – overlap with ADHD, so it makes it harder to see if a child with ADHD has depression. Because ADHD tends to make children underachieve, they can start to feel demoralised. However, depression is more than this. One study showed that children with ADHD, who have difficulty with social relationships, are more likely to suffer depression than those who are having general difficulties at school. Studies suggest up to a third of children with ADHD also have depression, and children who have ADHD are three times as likely to have depression as children who do not. Depression is also more likely to be missed in boys, because the symptoms of ADHD are more obvious than the symptoms of depression. Boys are also more likely to get into fights, cut themselves and steer clear of friends. Depression does not last any longer in a child with ADHD than a child without ADHD.

It is worth talking to a GP about the possibility of depression if you notice:

- The child has stopped doing the things they usually enjoy
- Their personality has changed
- They avoid friends and communicate less with you/significant care givers
- They seem unhappier than usual

Depression can be managed with several treatments:

- Cognitive Behavioural Therapy helps overcome negative thinking. It can also help the child to solve problems, do more things they like, and support them in learning better social skills.

- SSRIs are a type of antidepressant medication. SSRI stands for selective serotonin re-uptake inhibitor. All antidepressants have a delay of at least two weeks before they start to work, and often this delay can be up to six weeks. This early stage of treatment is when any side-effects are at their greatest, so persevering with treatment is important if these effects are tolerable. If the first antidepressant does not suit a particular child, a different one is worth trying. All antidepressants should be started gradually and taken for at least six months. The doctor will advise when the child is ready to come off medication. But antidepressants should be withdrawn slowly, over about six weeks.

In general, depression tends to last for less than nine months. Studies show that after a year, up to 80 per cent of children are better. However, 50 per cent of children with depression are likely to have another depressive episode within two months. Around 10 per cent of children with depression find their condition is persistent.

Appendix 4
Emotion Coaching Information

Emotion Coaching makes use of moments of heightened emotion and behaviour to guide and teach the child or young person about more effective responses. It is this process of empathetic engagement that enables the child to truly 'feel' validated and supported. This engenders a sense of security which, in turn, supports the child to calm down and engage in rational thinking and problem solving.

Porges (2011) highlights how prosody, eye gaze, facial expression and the body language of the adult can convey a sense of calmness and safety. This then allows for the dampening down of the vagus nerve's defensive system, thereby enabling the child to physiologically and psychologically calm down. The approach does not, in any sense, condone inappropriate behaviours, but encourages the child or young person to reflect upon them in a more rational and effective manner – once they have calmed down and are able to participate in the problem-solving process. The latter will generally make use of solution-focused strategies, with an emphasis on developing the child's ability to make use of key tools and frameworks that are age appropriate. Emotion Coaching requires practice, like any other set of skills, but clearly the results merit this level of hard work. Ultimately, it ensures that children and young people can and do effectively regulate their emotions, reduce their negative externalising behaviour and build their levels of resilience (Shortt *et al.*, 2010; Wilson *et al.*, 2012).

The five steps

Gottman and colleagues (1997) identified five steps that Emotion Coaching adults use with children and young people, as follows:

1 **Being aware of the child's emotion**
    Adults need to be aware of their own emotions prior to then becoming aware of those being experienced by the child or young person. Being emotionally literate is key here. This kind of emotional awareness involves recognising when you are feeling an emotion, the ability to identify the emotion, and sensitivity to the presence of emotions in others.

2 Recognising emotion as an opportunity for intimacy and teaching

Uncomfortable or negative experiences and emotions can serve as opportunities to empathise, build intimacy/connectivity with children and young people and teach them emotional skills. By acknowledging low-level or low intensity emotions, adults and children practise listening and problem-solving, and this is foundational for effective management of more intense emotions and the behaviours that may directly result.

3 Listening empathically and validating the child's feelings

This is a bit like taking a helicopter view of a situation as it unfolds. An adult needs to watch for physical evidence of a child's emotions and use their imagination to see the situation from the child's perspective, putting themselves in the child's shoes. The words they use then need to reflect back, in a soothing, non-critical manner, what they are seeing and hearing.

4 Helping the child verbally label the emotions

Teaching a vocabulary to label these emotions is essential in this process. Providing the words can help children transform what may be a scary, uncomfortable feeling or experience into something definable with boundaries. This, in turn, helps to normalise emotional experiences.

5 Setting limits while helping the child to problem-solve

This process can have five parts: 1. limit-setting (if appropriate); 2. identifying goals; 3. thinking of possible solutions; 4. evaluating proposed solutions; and 5. helping the child to choose a solution. What is important here is the focus on developing the child's skills and providing them with a key set of tools. This is both respectful and empowering, whilst also ensuring that the child can and does feel safe and boundaried.

Appendix 5
Using Circle of Friends Approaches

Circle of Friends, sometimes known as Circle of Support, is a powerful tool for inclusion and may be worth considering as a means of supporting more vulnerable and anxious children back into school.

The Circle of Friends approach works by developing a support network around individuals in the school community who are experiencing social difficulties often due to a specific disability, difference or behaviour. Volunteers from the peer group meet regularly with the target pupil therefore ensuring that relationships are built around him/her. The group also problem-solves with the target pupil in order to address any social and emotional difficulties that he/she may be experiencing in school. This approach has been used to great effect in many schools in order to ensure the inclusion of individual pupils with additional needs including mental health difficulties and social phobia. This is the rationale for including this as an Appendix in this publication.

The approach can be used to develop a sense of community in the class and the school. It is an important tool for enhancing the social cohesion of pupils and for ensuring that a class gels. In this way, it can be used to ensure a smooth transition from primary to secondary school. At certain points of transition, pupils need to find their own feet - but some may also need a supporting hand, which this approach can provide.

Main aims of the approach

The main aims of the approach are:

- To increase the level of acceptance and inclusion of pupils who are currently deemed to be excluded from the peer group.

- To harness and further develop the skills of pupils who are already considered to be highly skilled in terms of providing friendship and support to others.

- To encourage staff to reflect upon their own views and practices in order to develop more inclusive approaches, resources and policies.

- To impact positively upon whole school structures and systems by encouraging a review by the whole school community as to how these can be made more inclusive.

- To promote a cultured ethos of social support which encourages all staff and pupils to utilise and develop their own skills in terms of valuing and supporting others.

- To encourage the continued and ongoing use of 'support teams' in order to ensure the inclusion of all pupils in the school context.

- To further develop the social and emotional skills of those pupils identified as members of the group; for example, the ability to listen, to reflect, to evaluate, to empathise, to problem solve, to understand, to identify and to cope effectively with feelings (of self and others).

'SEMH' and social isolation

It is important to emphasise the fact that social, emotional and mental health difficulties go hand-in-hand with social isolation. These children have difficulty being accepted by peers because of their behaviour/social anxiety, and can behave even more inappropriately because they feel hurt and angry at being friendless.

The Circle of Friends process attempts to help students to make a link between feelings and behaviour. Members of the circles as 'potential friends'. If the process helps to turn these into real friends, and enhances the child's overall sense of self-worth as an individual, then it could also be a life changing experience.

How it works

Once the vulnerable child who is in need of peer support has been identified, the teacher/facilitator can arrange to conduct the introductory session with the whole class/form group (in the absence of the target child). The 'key' activity undertaken is to complete a Relationship Circles Activity. This involves children in thinking about the people in their lives - family, friends and acquaintances - and writing their names in a series of concentric circles. Instructions might be as follows:

1. Put the name of those you are closest to in circle 1, usually your family, sometimes described as people you live with or people you like to hug (people who love you most).

2. Your very best friends in circle 2 but not quite as close as circle 1.

3. Your wider friends in circle 3, maybe people in groups, scouts or a team.

4. Place those who are paid to help you in circle 4, these include people like doctors and teachers.

The circle diagram

Children are then encouraged to consider the target child and the fact that he/she is absent from the room. They are asked to think about his/her problems and possible lack of friends/difficulties in relating to or being with others/fears about being in a group due to these difficulties.

Then ideas can be recorded prior to children explaining their circle diagram to others and to specifically consider how they would feel if they had no one to place in circles 2 and 3.

Feelings are recorded and the children are then asked to consider how the target childt might be feeling and whether or not they may be able to help in supporting the child in forming a Circle of Friends.

Volunteers are then requested and a small group (6-8) is chosen by the facilitator/teacher to undertake this intervention. The facilitator then meets with the target child to explain that the group has been formed and that they will be supporting him/her in the following 6-8 weeks in order to further facilitate and ensure their inclusion.

The meetings

The first meeting is arranged for the following week in order to give those involved thinking time. It is at the first meeting the rules of the circle are decided,

At the start of the meeting, confidentiality is emphasised, and the times for subsequent meeting are set. The group decide upon a name but this should not involve the name of the focus student - the aim is to try to help the student become part of the circumference of the circle, but not the centre.

The kind of rules set are often similar to circle time: e.g. one person speaks at a time; everyone listens to each speaker; only constructive comments are allowed (although children may have to talk honestly about the behaviour of others, it must be done in a kind and positive way, often described as 'no put downs').

The children are assured that everything will take place in school time and that they are not to worry about problems brought up in the circle at home. During circle meetings the group talk with the target child about the good things they've seen him/her do that week. The child can then talk about any troubles he/she is having and how the group can give support, helping him/her to deal with difficult times in a more positive way. The group is encouraged to be honest, supportive and understanding. The development of empathy is clearly central here.

Key questions for the sessions might be posed as follows:

- What has gone well for the child this week?
- What have we, as his/her Circle of Friends observed?
- What hasn't gone quite so well?
- How can we help to change this?
- Does the child feel this is an accurate picture?
- What would he/she like support with?
- What strategies can we use?
- How will we measure our success and when will we do this, i.e. set the date!

A success story

When the teacher/facilitator effectively supports the Circle of Friends participants in delivering the intervention, positive outcomes can generally be expected. The target child will hopefully have gained in three key areas and be more able to:

- effectively manage his/her behaviour in school
- build positive relationships with peers
- improve his/her self-concept and self-esteem and well being.

The Circle of Friends group will also have benefitted in terms of developing their own pro-social skills, empathy, ability to analyse others' behaviour, and increased their awareness of the value and importance of including others in positive and meaningful relationships. As adults, we should never underestimate the latter.

Appendix 6
Trauma Recovery Self-Care Tips

This information sheet is designed to support adults who may be experiencing the effects of trauma or heightened levels of anxiety and highlights some essential self-care strategies.

Tip 1: Get moving

Trauma disrupts your body's natural equilibrium, freezing you in a state of hyper-arousal and fear. As well as burning off adrenaline and releasing endorphins, exercise and movement can help to repair your nervous system.

Try to exercise for 30 minutes or more on most days. Or, if it is easier, three 10-minute spurts of exercise per day are just as good.

Exercise that is rhythmic and engages both your arms and legs – such as walking, running, swimming, basketball, or even dancing – works best.

Add a Mindfulness element. Instead of focusing on your thoughts or distracting yourself while you exercise, really focus on your body and how it feels as you move. Notice the sensation of your feet hitting the ground, for example, or the rhythm of your breathing, or the feeling of wind on your skin. Rock climbing, boxing, weight training, or martial arts can make this easier – after all, you need to focus on your body movements during these activities in order to avoid injury.

Tip 2: Do not isolate

Following a trauma, you may want to withdraw from others, but isolation only makes things worse. Connecting to others face to face will help you heal, so try to maintain your relationships and avoid spending too much time alone.

You do not have to talk about the trauma. Connecting with others does not have to involve talking about the trauma. In fact, for some people, that can just make things worse. Comfort comes from feeling engaged and accepted by others.

Ask for support. While you do not have to talk about the trauma itself, it is important that you have someone to share your feelings with face to face, someone who will listen attentively without judging you. Turn to a trusted family member, friend, or counsellor.

Participate in social activities, even if you do not feel like it. Do 'normal' activities with other people, activities that have nothing to do with the traumatic experience.

Reconnect with old friends. If you have retreated from relationships that were once important to you, make the effort to reconnect.

Join a support group. Connecting with others who are facing the same problems can help reduce your sense of isolation and hearing how others cope can help inspire you in your own recovery.

Volunteer. As well as helping others, volunteering can be a great way to challenge the sense of helplessness that often accompanies trauma. Remind yourself of your strengths and reclaim your sense of power by helping others.

Make new friends. If you live alone or far from family and friends, it's important to reach out and make new friends. Take a class or join a club to meet people with similar interests, connect to an alumni association, or reach out to neighbours or work colleagues.

If connecting to others is difficult … Many people who have experienced trauma feel disconnected, withdrawn and find it difficult to connect with other people. If that describes you, there are some actions you can take before you next meet with a friend:

- **Exercise or move.** Jump up and down, swing your arms and legs, or just flail around. Your head will feel clearer and you will find it easier to connect.

- **Vocal toning.** As strange as it sounds, vocal toning is a great way to open up to social engagement. Sit up straight and simply make 'mmmm' sounds. Change the pitch and volume until you experience a pleasant vibration in your face.

Tip 3: Self-regulate your nervous system

No matter how agitated, anxious, or out of control you feel, it is important to know that you can change your arousal system and calm yourself. Not only will it help relieve the anxiety associated with trauma, but it will also engender a greater sense of control.

Mindful breathing. If you are feeling disoriented, confused, or upset, practising mindful breathing is a quick way to calm yourself. Simply take 60 breaths, focusing your attention on each 'out' breath.

Sensory input. Does a specific sight, smell or taste quickly make you feel calm? Or maybe petting an animal or listening to music works to quickly soothe you? Everyone responds to sensory input a little differently, so experiment with different quick stress relief techniques to find what works best for you.

Staying grounded. To feel in the present and more grounded, sit on a chair. Feel your feet on the ground and your back against the chair. Look around you and pick six objects that have red or blue in them. Notice how your breathing gets deeper and calmer.

Allow yourself to feel what you feel when you feel it. Acknowledge your feelings about the trauma as they arise and accept them.

Tip 4: Take care of your health

It is true: having a healthy body can increase your ability to cope with the stress of trauma.

Get plenty of sleep. After a traumatic experience, worry or fear may disturb your sleep patterns. But a lack of quality sleep can exacerbate your trauma symptoms and make it harder to maintain your emotional balance. Go to sleep and get up at the same time each day and aim for seven to nine hours of sleep each night.

Avoid alcohol and drugs. Their use can worsen your trauma symptoms and increase feelings of depression, anxiety, and isolation.

Eat a well-balanced diet. Eating small, well-balanced meals throughout the day will help you keep your energy up and minimise mood swings. Avoid sugary and fried foods and eat plenty of omega-3 fats – such as salmon, walnuts, soybeans, and flaxseeds – to give your mood a boost.

Reduce stress. Try relaxation techniques such as meditation, yoga, or deep breathing exercises. Schedule time for activities that bring you joy such as your favourite hobbies or creative activities.

Appendix 7
Whole School Recovery

Building schools to foster recovery & heal

Given what we now know about the impact of trauma and the fact that we are all living through a complex and multi-faceted trauma at this time, it is also clear that our schools will need to incorporate therapeutic approaches and in essence 'be therapeutic'. This does not mean that they must take on the role of CAMHS, but it does mean that they need to recognise their own potential to support the healing process and ensure post-traumatic growth.

The school community itself is the medicine in our view. Schools will need to provide the safe and nurturing haven that children need. Ensuring those who are the most vulnerable have the wrap-around care they need will be paramount, but so too will be the need to ensure that **all** in the community feel safe and held. Building resilience does not happen by accident. We need to make it happen.

Supporting children who are volatile, jumpy, nervous, scared, hyper-vigilant or withdrawn, or in survival mode is something we will all need to be aware of and confident in doing. This only happens when we accept the evidence from neuroscience, act on it and ensure that **we** have regulated nervous systems to meet such demands, not becoming overwhelmed and burnt out ourselves.

Creating the healing context

School staff may wish to consider the following ideas in terms of developing a healing context in which children can begin to recover:

- Holding celebrations/memorials to celebrate carers/NHS staff or simply the school community itself. It is important to make use of such opportunities to reinforce the power and resilience of the community as a whole and to ensure that everyone feels held and safe. Remember that we can all find meaning and gain knowledge within a communal crisis, and allowing this to happen gives a powerful message to children that we are not alone in this – genuinely. This is particularly important when many of us will have felt very alone and isolated during the lockdown process, without access to this kind of communal support.

- Reinforce the importance of social buffering (Kikusui *et al.*, 2006), whereby social contact appears to have an incredibly positive influence on the psychological and the physiological aspects of social animals, including us human beings. Relationships need to be the centre of all we do. Ensuring that we connect with those who find it the hardest to connect – both children and adults – will be crucial. In simple terms – kindness will need to rule! Keeping lines of honest communication open and sharing our experiences and feelings will be important for all of us in order to feel contained and to provide this buffering for the most vulnerable.

- Flexibility will also be needed. Some will require more support and more specialised input. We need to make sure that assessment processes and identification tools are used across the school to identify those most at risk and to act at the outset to provide the support that they may need. Many will find getting back to school an emotional trauma in itself, so ensuring that staff are aware of how to manage issues such as school phobia and how to support on an individual and wider basis will also be necessary. Flexibility around gradual attendance and engagement for some children will need to be part of this approach, alongside individualised opportunities to engage in self-regulation. Children will not learn without this and trying to push them into academic learning and larger social contexts when they are unable to cope carries the risk of reinforcing and reliving their trauma. Gradual desensitisation to their fears and getting back to routines and structures will be the way forward.

- Listening authentically and with empathy needs to permeate all we do. Children may feel frightened and overwhelmed by leaving home and going into a social context – however well distanced – given the reinforcement they had received over months regarding the dangers of contracting the virus. This is the essential therapeutic approach. It is healing in itself – to talk, to feel heard and to feel safe. We need to provide time for this, as and when needed. This does not equate to taking on the role of the therapist, but does mean that we can *all* be more therapeutic in our interactions. In this way, we make pain tolerable and not toxic.

- Reinforcing safety rules, boundaries and consistent approaches will help to reduce toxic stress. New rules around social distancing need to be framed as 'dos' rather than 'don'ts', as this helps to reduce anxiety by framing the rules as positive and protective of ourselves and each other. Order, calm and reassurance need to be paramount.

- Giving time to reflect on what we value is also important, given that most of us will have spent some time doing just that during these stressful times. We may well have come to a new realisation as to what really matters, what we value and what is essential and important to us in our lives. Children need to talk about this too. What is it they want now from their school community, and how can it be better, more empathic, more inclusive, kinder? This is something to celebrate and hold on to – our children's resourcefulness and vision. **We are creating a 'new normal', so perhaps this is our chance to make it better than the old one.**

Appendix 8
A Recovery Plan to Support School Staff and Carers as Children Return to School

Recovery and rebuilding our connections are now essential and building and **maintaining emotional wellbeing** must be the *key focus* for all.

Encourage a focus on our *values and strengths* highlighting the positives, what we have learnt, what went well and could work again – give **HOPE**.

Co-regulation is essential so ensure that **ALL** staff and CYP can develop their own *toolbox of strategies* and have the chance to use and develop them daily.

Observe and *acknowledge changes/losses/bereavements* knowing the *grief is unique and not linear* and relationships help us to heal.

Value the staff team and put their wellbeing first remembering that unregulated adults cannot support /nurture unregulated CYP - They need their **CALM** so provide whole school systems/peer support/interventions that work.

Explain that education is a lifelong journey – 'you may have missed bits/feel worried about being behind, but we are here to help you and know how to do it – we all have more than one chance and this is not a race but a journey for us all'

Repair for those who need it is an essential – this does not mean a bespoke therapeutic intervention for all but remembering that *every conversation can be an intervention* – so listen, acknowledge uncertainty, be curious and kind.

Yesterdays are there to be learnt from – we all have worries, fears, concerns and we have all made mistakes – be *solution focused* now identifying what we have learnt, what we can do differently in this new normal and how we can co-create new solutions together.

Plan the welcome for all and reaffirm the routines and safety measures – 'we are here to keep you safe and we can do this together' creating a *shared mission* – **this is a SAFE SPACE for you.**

Learn from their experiences – *the voice of the child is paramount* – 'I need help with this, I am worried about this, I can't do this anymore' - NOT 'this is what you need from us adults right now'.

Attachments matter – reaffirm these showing that we care, value, and want to be together – *these relationships can and do ensure post traumatic growth.*

Nurture for all within a *resilient, flexible, and compassionate community* will pave the way for wellbeing, engagement and success in **all** domains so **let's 'catch up' with 'Real Recovery'** knowing that we **CAN** do this together.

References

American Psychological Association (APA), 2012, 'Building Your Resilience'. Retrieved 9.8.20. from https://www.apa.org/topics/resilience.

Appleyard Carmody K., Egeland B., van Dulmen M. & Sroufe L.A., 2005, 'When More is Not Better: The role of cumulative risk in child behavior outcomes', Journal of Child Psychology and Psychiatry 46(3), pp235–45.

Borba M., 2003, *Esteem Builders: A K-8 self-esteem curriculum for improving student achievement, behaviour and school climate*, Jalmar Press, San Francisco.

Golding K., 2013, Nurturing Attachments Training Resource: Running parenting groups for adoptive parents and foster or kinship carers, Jessica Kingsley, London.

Gottman J., 1997, *Raising an Emotionally Intelligent Child*, Simon & Schuster New York.

Hughes D. & Baylin J., 2013, Brain-Based Parenting: The neuroscience of caregiving for healthy attachment, W.W.Norton, New York.

Kikusui T., Winslow J.T. & Mori Y., 2006, 'Social Buffering: Relief from stress and anxiety', *Philosophical Transactions of the Royal Society of Biological Sciences* 361(1476), pp2215–28. DOI: 10.1098/rstb.2006.1941.

van der Kolk B., 2003, 'The Neurobiology of Childhood Trauma and Abuse', Child & Adolescent Psychiatric Clinics of North America 12, pp293–317.

OFSTED, 2020, *COVID-19 series: briefing on schools Evidence from pilot visits to schools between 29 September and 23 October 2020*, October 2020

Perry B., 24 April 2020, *9. Managing Transitions: Neurosequential Network Stress & Trauma Series 2020*, Video file, InfoNMN. Retrieved from https://www.youtube.com/watch?v=cA7UbKnM0RM&feature=youtu.be.

Porges S.W., 2011, *The Polyvagal Theory: Neurophysiological foundations of emotions, attachment, communication, and self-regulation*, Norton Series on Interpersonal Neurobiology, W.W. Norton & Co, New York.

References

Rae T., 2016, *Building Positive Thinking Habits: Increasing self-confidence and resilience in young people through CBT*, Hinton House Publishers, Buckingham.

Rae, T., Walshe, J. & Wood, J. 2017, *The Essential Guide to using Mindfulness with Young)eople* Buckingham: Hinton House Publishers

Rae T., Bunn H. &. Walshe J., 2018, *The Essential Guide to Using Positive Psychology with Children and Young People*, Hinton House Publishers, Buckingham.

Rae T., Such A. & Wood J., 2020, *The Wellbeing Toolkit for Mental Health Leads in Schools: A comprehensive training resource to support emotional wellbeing in education and social care*, Hinton House Publishers, Buckingham.

Rae, T., 2020, *A Toolbox of Wellbeing Helpful strategies and activities for children, teens, their carers and teachers* Buckingham: Hinton House Publishers

Shortt J.W., Stoolmiller M., Smith-Shine J.N., Eddy J.M. & Sheeber L., 2010, 'Maternal Emotion Coaching, Adolescent Anger Regulation, and Siblings' Externalizing Symptoms', *Journal of Child Psychology & Psychiatry* 51.7, pp799–808.

Sroufe A., Egeland B., Carlson E. & Collins A., 2005, *The Development of the Person: The Minnesota study of risk and adaptation from birth to adulthood*, Guildford Press, New York.

Tedeschi R. & Calhoun L., 2004, 'Posttraumatic Growth: Conceptual foundations and empirical evidence', *Psychological Inquiry* 15(1), pp1–18.

Torre J.B. & Lieberman M.D., 2018, 'Putting Feelings into Words: Affect labeling as implicit emotion regulation', *Emotion Review* 10(2), pp116–24.

Wilson K.R., Havighurst S.S. & Harley A.E., 2012, 'Tuning into Kids: An effectiveness trial of a parenting program targeting emotion socialization of preschoolers', *Journal of Family Psychology* 26.1, pp56–65.

Young Minds, 2020, 'Coronavirus: The impact on young people with mental health needs', https://youngminds.org.uk/about-us/reports/coronavirus-impact-on-young-people-with-mental-health-needs/